Civil Procedure in Egypt

Civil Procedure in Egypt

Second Edition

Fathi Waly

This book was originally published as a monograph in the International Encyclopaedia of Laws/Civil Procedure.

Founding Editor: Roger Blanpain
General Editor: Frank Hendrickx
Volume Editor: Piet Taelman

Wolters Kluwer

Published by:
Kluwer Law International B.V.
PO Box 316
2400 AH Alphen aan den Rijn
The Netherlands
E-mail: international-sales@wolterskluwer.com
Website: lrus.wolterskluwer.com

Sold and distributed in North, Central and South America by:
Wolters Kluwer Legal & Regulatory U.S.
7201 McKinney Circle
Frederick, MD 21704
United States of America
Email: customer.service@wolterskluwer.com

Sold and distributed in all other countries by:
Air Business Subscriptions
Rockwood House
Haywards Heath
West Sussex
RH16 3DH
United Kingdom
Email: international-customerservice@wolterskluwer.com

ISBN 978-94-035-2564-8

e-Book: ISBN 978-94-035-2565-5
web-PDF: ISBN 978-94-035-2570-9

The Author

Fathi Waly was the Dean of the Faculty of Law, Vice-President of Cairo University, Head of Department of Civil Procedure, for many years. He is now an attorney at the Court of Cassation in Egypt, Professor of Civil Procedure at Cairo University and the Head of the Egyptian Society for Civil and Commercial Procedure. He participated in the drafting committee for the Egyptian Code of Civil Procedure and in the drafting committee for the Egyptian new law of arbitration. He also has participated in drafting the Code of Civil and Commercial Procedure in Kuwait and in Palestine.

He is the author of many books. The most important are: Theory of Nullity in Civil Procedures (1959–1997); The Enforcement in Civil and Commercial Matters (several editions from 1962 to 1995); Law of Civil Justice in Egypt (several editions from 1973 to 2009); Law of Civil Justice in Lebanon (1969); Law of Civil Justice in Kuwait (1974); The Enforcement in Civil and Commercial Matters in Lebanon (1970); The Enforcement in Civil and Commercial Matters in Kuwait (1975); Arbitration Law (2007); Arbitration in National and Commercial International Litigations (2014); Writings on Civil Justice and Arbitration (Notes and Articles published in legal reviews, 1961–2014) (2015); Treatise of Law of Civil Justice (two volumes – 2017). He has published several articles in Arabic, English and Italian.

Table of Contents

The Author 3

List of Abbreviations 13

General Introduction 15

§1. General Background 15

§2. Delimitation of the Subject Matter 16

§3. Sources of Civil Procedure Law 16

§4. Characteristics of the Egyptian Civil Procedure 16

§5. Fundamental Guarantees of Justice 17
I. Publicity of Judicial Debates 17
II. The Independence of the Judiciary 17
A. The Irremovability of Judges 18
B. The Superior Council of the Judiciary 18
C. Principle of Free Access to Justice 18

Part I. Judicial Organization 19

Chapter 1. The Courts and Their Members 19

§1. Courts 19

§2. Members of the Judiciary 22
I. Appointment of Magistrates 22
II. Career of Magistrates 23
III. Discipline 23
IV. Incompatibilities 24

Chapter 2. The Legal Profession 25

§1. Exercise of the Legal Profession 25
I. Conditions for Admission 25

§2. Rights and Duties 25

§3. Discipline 26

§4. The Bar 27

Chapter 3. Officials of the Courts 28

§1. Clerks 28

§2. Bailiffs 28

Part II. Jurisdiction 31

Chapter 1. Domestic Jurisdiction 31

§1. Subject Matter Jurisdiction 31
I. Tribunal of Grand Instance (*Mahkama Kulia*) 31
II. Tribunal of Small Instance (*Mahkama Guzeea*) 31
III. Jurisdiction for Urgent Cases 31

§2. Territorial Jurisdiction (Venue) 32

§3. Adjustments of Jurisdiction Rules 34

§4. Resolution of Jurisdiction Conflicts 35

Chapter 2. International Jurisdiction 37

§1. Rules Applicable in the Absence of a Treaty 37
I. Privilege of Jurisdiction for Egyptian Nationals in Egyptian Courts 37
II. Jurisdiction for Claims Against a Foreigner Who Has No Domicile or Residence in Egypt 37
III. Jurisdiction for Successions 38
IV. Extension of International Jurisdiction 38
V. Domestic Rules of Territorial Jurisdiction Applied to International Disputes 38
VI. Resolution of Jurisdictional Conflicts 39

§2. International Treaties 39

Part III. Actions, Claims and Defences 41

Chapter 1. The Judicial Action 41

§1. DEFINITION 41

§2. CONDITIONS OF THE RIGHT OF ACTION 42

§3. ADMISSIBILITY OF THE ACTION (INTEREST IN THE ACTION) 42

§4. VEXATION LITIGATION 44

Chapter 2. Claims and Defences 45

§1. CLAIMS 45

§2. DEFENCES 45
I. Defence on Merits 45
II. Procedural Exceptions 45
III. Demurers 46

Chapter 3. Sanctions on Procedural Irregularities 47

§1. NULLITY OF ACTS OF PROCEDURE 47
I. Cases in Which the Nullification Is Granted 47
A. Nullity Due to a Defect in Form 47
B. Substantive Nullity 47
II. Rules of Nullity 48

§2. LAPSE OF THE PROCEDURAL RIGHT 48

Part IV. Proceedings 49

Chapter 1. Conciliation Before Trial 49

Chapter 2. Proceedings in First Instance 51

§1. PRINCIPLES GOVERNING A LAWSUIT 51
I. Principle of the Demand 51
II. Principle of Adversary Proceedings 51

§2. ORDINARY PROCEEDINGS 52
I. Introduction of the Instance 52
II. Progress of Proceedings 54
III. Judgment 55
IV. Judgment by Default 57

Chapter 3. Challenge of Judgments 59

§1. GENERAL PRINCIPLES 59

§2. Appeal 60
I. Conditions to Appeal 60
II. Appeal Proceedings 60
III. Effects of Appeal 61

§3. Petition for Review 62
I. Reasons of Petition for Review 63
II. Effects of the Petition 63
III. Proceedings for the Petition for Review 64

§4. Cassation 64
I. Nature of the Challenge of Cassation 64
II. Reasons of Cassation 64
III. Judgments Challenged by Cassation 65
IV. Proceedings in the Court of Cassation 65
V. Effects of the Challenge of Cassation 66
VI. Effects of the Quashing of a Judgment 66

§5. Opposition by a Third Person 67

Part V. Incidents 69

§1. Joinder of Actions 69

§2. Discontinuance of the Instance 69

§3. Suspension of the Instance 70

§4. Termination of the Instance 70
I. Expiration of the Instance 70
II. Time Limitation 71
III. Withdrawal of the Instance 71

Part VI. Legal Costs and Legal Aids 73

Chapter 1. Legal Costs 73

Chapter 2. Legal Aid 74

Part VII. Evidence 75

Chapter 1. Burden of Proof 76

Chapter 2. The Judge's Authority 77

Chapter 3. Admissibility of Evidence 78

Chapter 4. Administration of Evidence 79

§1. Written Proof 79

§2. Production of Written Papers 80

§3. Witness Evidence 81

§4. Questioning of the Parties 82

§5. Proof by Oath 83
I. Decisive Oath 83
II. Completive Oath 84

§6. View of Premises 84

§7. Expert Evidence 85

Part VIII. Particular Proceedings 87

Chapter 1. Non-contentious Matters 88

Chapter 2. Orders of Payment 90

Part IX. Enforcement of Judgments and Preliminary Seizure for Security 93

Chapter 1. General Rules 94

§1. The Judge of Execution and the Execution Officer 94
I. The Execution's Administration 94
II. The Judge of Execution 94
III. The Execution Officer 94

§2. The Enforceable Instruments 95

§3. The Judicial Judgment as an Enforceable Instrument 95

§4. Object of Seizure 96

§5. Preliminary Seizure for Security 96

§6. Judgment of Validity and Efficacy of Provisional Seizure 97

Chapter 2. Proceedings 98

§1. Kinds of Seizure 98

§2. Seizure of Rights or of Movable Material Properties Possessed by a Third Person 98

§3. Seizure of Movable Material Properties Possessed by the Debtor 99

§4. Seizure of Shares, Bonds and Revenues 100

§5. Seizure of Real Property 100

§6. Distribution of the Proceeds of the Enforcement 102

Chapter 3. Recognition and Enforcement of Foreign Judgments 103

Part X. Arbitration 105

Chapter 1. Introduction 105

Chapter 2. Arbitrability 106

Chapter 3. Arbitration Agreement and Party Autonomy 107

§1. General 107

§2. The Arbitration Compromise and the Arbitration Clause 108

§3. Arbitration Concerning Administrative Contracts 109

§4. Legal Effects of the Arbitral Agreement 109

§5. Competence of Competence 110

Chapter 4. Arbitral Tribunal 111

§1. Nomination of the Arbitrators 111

§2. Challenge of Arbitrators 112

§3. Termination of the Arbitrator's Mission 112

Chapter 5. Interim Measures and Preliminary Awards 114

§1. PARTIAL AWARD 114

§2. PRELIMINARY ARBITRATION AWARD 114

§3. TEMPORAL OR EXPEDITED ARBITRATION AWARD 115

§4. INTERIM MEASURES 116

Chapter 6. Conduct of Arbitral Proceedings 119

§1. NON-CONFORMITY TO THE STATE COURT PROCEEDINGS 119

§2. EGYPTIAN ARBITRATION LAW PROCEDURES 119
I. Commencement of Proceedings 119
II. Place of Arbitration 119
III. Language of Arbitration 120
IV. The Claimant's Statement 120
V. Respondent's Memorandum of Defence 120
VI. Submission of Documents 121
VII. Notification of Notices and Papers 121
VIII. Pleading Sessions 121
IX. The Discontinuation of the Arbitration Instance 122
X. The Suspension of the Arbitration Instance 122

Chapter 7. Evidence Before the Arbitral Tribunal 123

§1. GENERAL RULES 123

§2. EXPERTISE 123

Chapter 8. Ending of the Arbitral Proceedings 124

§1. ORDER OF ENDING BY THE ARBITRAL TRIBUNAL 124

§2. ORDER OF ENDING BY THE PRESIDENT OF THE STATE COURT 124

Chapter 9. Arbitral Award 125

§1. THE TIME LIMIT 125

§2. APPLICABLE LAW 125

§3. THE RENDERING OF THE AWARD 126

§4. The Discharging of the Arbitral Tribunal 126
I. Interpretation of the Awards 127
II. Correction of Material Mistakes 127
III. Completion of the Award 127

Chapter 10. Nullity of the Award 128

§1. Cases of Nullity of the Award 128

§2. Jurisdiction and Time Limit 128

Chapter 11. Enforcement of the Arbitration Award 130

Selected Bibliography 133

Index 135

List of Abbreviations

Arb.L	Arbitration Law
Art.	Article
C.C.Proc.	Code of Civil Procedure
Eg. Con.	Egyptian Constitution
Civ.C.	Civil Code
Ed.	Edition
L	Law
L. Evidence	Law of Evidence
L.J.Auth.	Law of Judicial Authority
S.C.J.	Superior Council of the Judiciary

General Introduction

§1. General Background

1. Egypt is a civil state. The religion of the state and of the majority of its population is Islam (about 90% of the population).

According to the new Egyptian Constitution of 2014, the regime is a compromise between a parliamentary regime and a presidential one. The Parliament consists of one House called 'Counsel of representatives' (Article 101 Eg. Con.).

The main source of legislation should be the principles of Sharia (Islamic Law) (Article 2 Eg. Con.). The basic principle of the Arabic Republic of Egypt is a socialist democratic regime. The Egyptian people are part of the Arabic nation and aim towards the complete entity of it. The official language is the Arabic language (Article 2 Eg. Con.).

2. The Egyptian judicial power proclaims the rule of law through the courts. These are divided into two orders:

(1) Administrative Courts which deal with contentious matters between individuals and public authorities.
(2) Judicial Courts which are divided into two branches – criminal courts and civil courts (*largo sensu*).

Apart from these two different orders, Egypt has the 'Supreme Constitutional Court' which has been established according to Article 174 Eg. Con. by Law No. 48/1979. It controls the conformity of the laws and decrees to the rules of the Constitution.

Besides those two orders, the new constitution added a third order which is the Military Jurisdiction, as an independent jurisdiction (Article 204 Eg. Con.) to judge all crimes related to military forces, officers and other military members, during their service or related to it.

According to Article 204/2 Eg. Con., it is not allowed to judge a civilian before military courts unless they commit a direct crime against military premises or in military zones, or commit a direct offence to officers or soldiers during their service.

Members of military courts have the same immunities as the members of Judicial Authority (Article 204/4 Eg. Con.).

§2. Delimitation of the Subject Matter

3. Administrative courts have their own rules of procedure, although they draw their inspiration from the general principles of the Code of Civil and Commercial Procedure.

Criminal courts have their own rules of procedure, which can be found in the Code of Criminal Procedure (Law No. 150/1950).

Besides the rules of the Code of Civil and Commercial Procedure, Law No. 1/2000 concerning some of the procedures in family affairs contains some special procedural rules which apply in the absence of an applicable provision in the Code of Civil Procedure.

The civil procedure followed by civil courts in civil and commercial matters is only the subject matter of the present monograph.

§3. Sources of Civil Procedure Law

4. The present Code of Civil Procedure came into force on 10 November 1968. It has been amended partially from time to time by several laws; the most important are Law No. 23/1992, Law No. 18/1999. Law No. 76/2007, and Law No. 120/2008.

The matter of civil procedure in Egypt lies within the competence of the parliament. The government may not promulgate decrees to establish or modify civil procedure.

The present Code replaced an old one dating from 1949. The latter replaced two codes dating from 1875 (for Mixed Courts) and 1883 (for National Courts).

5. The Codes of 1875 and 1883 had inspired the Napoleonic Code of Civil Procedure.

The Code of 1949 had inspired the same rules as modified and clarified by French and Egyptian doctrine and jurisprudence.

The present Code had kept most of the rules of the Code of 1949 adding some rules from German and Italian doctrine and from the Italian Code of Civil Procedure of 1941, besides some thoughts of Egyptian authors and of the Egyptian Court of Cassation's decisions.

Law No. 120/2008 has established a new system for new courts called Economic Courts aiming to expedite the procedure for economic cases.

§4. Characteristics of the Egyptian Civil Procedure

6. The Procedure of the Codes of 1875/1883 was an adversary. The parties conducted the proceedings of a case by themselves or by their representatives; the judge considered himself neutral. The parties or their representatives brought forward to him the alleged facts and their evidence. The judge had no power to order ex officio a measure of investigation.

7. This adversary system has been changed gradually by both the Code of 1949 and the present Code of 1968.

The present Code presents a compromise between an adversary system and an inquisitorial one. According to the present Code, the judge intervenes in the administrating and in the management of the procedures. He may deliver ex officio an order for evidence, such as to hear witnesses, to question parties, or to produce documents. He may introduce into the process a person other than the parties. He is responsible for setting time-limits, for pleadings, for controlling the discovery of documents, or for closing the proceedings.

As far as the law is concerned, the judge is obliged to qualify the facts, and to search the law applicable to these facts, even if not brought forward by the parties.

8. This does not mean that civil procedure in Egypt has become inquisitorial. The party commences the procedure, brings forward the alleged facts, submits the legal evidence, qualifies the facts, and states his claims, which may not be altered by the judge. The parties may also put an end to the dispute.

§5. Fundamental Guarantees of Justice

I. Publicity of Judicial Debates

9. Article 187 Eg. Con. and Article 101 C.C.Proc. declare the principle of publicity of debates.

The publicity of debates is ensured by the opening of the court to the public, by the right of every person, even if not a party, to obtain a copy of the audience record, by the right of the media to publish both the pleadings and the sentences.

The publicity of debates does not mean necessarily the opening of the court to the public without limitation. The size of the court's accommodation may oblige the judge to limit the number of people who may attend the audience.

On the other hand, the judge may decide that the hearing be conducted 'in camera' if publicity would hurt the family's privacy or public interest or morals. In some cases, the law itself requires that hearings will be conducted without publicity, especially in family matters.

In all cases, even if the hearings are conducted without publicity, the judgment has to be pronounced in public (Article 187 Eg. Con. & Article 174 C.C.Proc.).

The sanction for lack of public hearing or public judgment is the nullity of the judgment. This nullity relates to public interest. Therefore, it can be raised at any stage of the procedure even for the first time in appeal or in cassation.

II. The Independence of the Judiciary

10. The Judiciary in Egypt is an independent power (Article 184 Eg. Con.). Judges, as members of this independent power, are independent. Article 166 of the Egyptian Constitution provides that 'Judges are independent, there is no authority upon their judgments except for the Law. No authority may interfere in the cases or in the matters of justice'. They are thus protected from the whims of the executive. To ensure this independence, the Constitution provides some institutions and principles as follows.

A. *The Irremovability of Judges*

11. Article 186 Eg. Con. provides that 'Judges may not be removed'. This principle extends to all judges sitting either in administrative courts or in judicial courts. It also extends to all members of the public ministry, and to military judges (Article 204 Eg. Con.).

The irremovability of judges means that they may not be removed, suspended, placed in retirement prematurely or moved to another court for causes unspecified by the law and without abiding by legal proceedings which should guarantee the independence of the Jurisdiction and the judges (Article 186 Eg. Con.).

B. *The Superior Council of the Judiciary*

12. The establishment of this council is the main guarantee of the independence of the judiciary. This council controls the nomination, the promotion and the movement from one court to another, punishment and all other matters concerning judges and members of the public ministry (Article 77*bis2*. L.J.Auth.). The council is chaired by the President of the Court of Cassation and comprises six members chosen according to their posts: President of the Cairo Court of Appeal, the Public Minister, the two most senior Vice-Presidents of the Court of Cassation, the two most senior Presidents of the Courts of Appeal (Article 77*bis1*. L.J.Auth.).

This Superior Council of the Judiciary (S.C.J.) deals with the affairs of the judicial judges. Judges of administrative courts have their own council (Private Council of the Council of State) which has the same competence for administrative judges (Article 68*bis*1 Law No. 47/1972).

C. *Principle of Free Access to Justice*

13. According to Article 97 Eg. Con. everyone has the right to access to justice. This access is open to all persons, whether Egyptians or foreigners. The Egyptian Constitution also provides that all citizens are equal before law disregarding their sex, origin, religion or faith (Article 40 Eg. Con.) and equal before justice (Article 53 Eg. Con.). This means that any citizen has an equal right to be judged by the same courts according to the same rules of the procedure without any discrimination.

Access to Egyptian courts is free, which means that litigants do not pay judges, clerks of the court, bailiffs or experts. All these are paid by the state. This does not mean that parties do not pay any expenses. The litigant who goes to court has to pay.

Part I. Judicial Organization

Chapter 1. The Courts and Their Members

§1. Courts

14. The judicial order, either civil or criminal, is composed of courts. The same courts, in different formations, are in charge of both civil and criminal matters. Each civil court is divided into specialized chambers. All chambers are composed of professional judges.

Specialized tribunals of small instances are sometimes designated to handle certain types of litigation, involving labour cases, execution of enforceable instruments and urgent matters.

On the other hand, Egypt does not have commercial courts, but only commercial chambers (except in Cairo and Alexandria where there is a commercial tribunal for small instances). Commercial tribunals in Cairo and Alexandria were established by two decrees from the Minister of Justice in 1940. They are not structurally separate courts but branches of the ordinary courts. But, these commercial chambers and tribunals are also composed of professional judges and follow the same procedure as in civil cases.

Besides, by Law No. 120/2008, Egypt knows now a new type of Courts called Economic Courts. They have a different structure as well as different procedures.

15. For civil cases, the principle of double layer of jurisdiction prevails. The dispute after a first trial in an inferior court (first instance) passes to the second trial in a higher court.

The principle of double layer is provided by Article 219 of the Code of Civil Procedure, but the Egyptian Constitution does not mention it.

This principle has some exceptions. The law does not permit the appeal of judgments in cases for small claims not exceeding EGP 5,000 in a court of small instance, or not exceeding EGP 40,000 in a court of grand instance.

16. The ordinary first instance court is called Tribunal of Grand Instance 'Mahkama Kolea'. There is one in the capital of each department. (Two in Cairo: one for southern Cairo, the other for northern Cairo.)

Each chamber of the Tribunal of Grand Instance is composed of three judges. The Tribunal of Grand Instance is competent in all civil, commercial, labour and family cases. In brief, it is competent in all civil (*in sensu largo*) cases except those given to another court.

17. In the district of every police office division (*Kessem*), there is a Tribunal of Small Instance competent in small cases (in which the claim does not exceed EGP 40,000) and of other specific cases. The chamber in a Tribunal of Small Instance is composed of one single judge. The chambers of the Tribunal of Grand Instance and the Tribunals of Small Instance in the same district are administered by the President of the Tribunal of Grand Instance who has the rank of a counsellor.

18. At the level of the second layer of jurisdiction, there are two kinds of courts. The Court of Appeal, hearing appeals of judgments of Tribunals of Grand Instance. There are nine Courts of Appeal in Egypt, in Cairo and in other main cities. The Court of Appeal comprises many chambers. Each chamber of the Court of Appeal is composed of three judges (the President and two members). For each Court of Appeal, there is a President who is the senior judge in the court (amended by Law No. 142/2006).

Judgments of tribunals of small instances are appealed to chambers in the Tribunal of Grand Instance. These chambers are called Appellate Chambers of the Tribunal of Grand Instance. Each chamber is composed of three judges, just like the other chambers in the same court.

19. A clerk always assists judges and counsellors, he who 'holds the pen'. The clerks of the court are civil servants, under the authority of the Ministry of Justice. Clerks have no adjudication powers, but the presence of a clerk is essential for the validity of the trial.

20. Besides judges who have the authority to adjudge, there is also the public minister. In criminal cases, his role is that of public prosecutor. In civil cases, the public minister also has an important role. He may raise an action in some cases, for instance, an action of bankruptcy (Article 76 Law No. 11/2018 on bankruptcy). In some cases, he is obliged to intervene to present his opinion about the case. In others, he may or may not intervene according to what he considers necessary for the protection of public interest.

The members of the public minister and the judges belong to the same body. They may pass from the bench to the floor and conversely in the course of their careers.

21. At the top of the courts of jurisdiction, there is a Court of Cassation. The Egyptian Court of Cassation was established in 1931, and it is the highest civil and criminal court. It is not a third degree of jurisdiction because it does not examine facts; it only controls the conformity of the decision with the rule of law. It checks how facts have been termed in law.

If the decision is not in conformity with the rule of law, it quashes it and transfers the case back to the Court of Appeal to be tried again in another chamber.

22. The Court of Cassation rules without transferring the case in three exceptional cases:

(1) If a decision concerning the same case is quashed twice.

(2) If after quashing the decision, the Court of Cassation finds the merit ready to be judged. In these two exceptions, the Court of Cassation judges the dispute as if it was a tribunal of merits.
(3) If the Court of Cassation quashes the decision for the incompetence of the tribunal which pronounced the decision. In this case, the court does not determine the competent tribunal or transfer the case to it.

Besides, the Court of Cassation rules on the merits if the challenged decision has been issued by an Economic Court according to Law No. 120/2008.

23. The Court of Cassation is made up of many chambers: civil, commercial, social, economic, or criminal.

The court is under the authority of a President who is at the top of the judicial hierarchy. Each chamber is presided over by a Vice-President. Some chambers have as many as seven judges; however, each chamber operates as a five-man court. If a civil or commercial chamber intends to disagree in its decision with a stable legal principle followed by civil and commercial chambers of the court, it should refer the case to the general assembly of civil and commercial matters which is composed of eleven members. This general assembly rules with the majority of seven judges.

In the event that one of the civil or commercial chambers disagrees with stable legal principle followed by penal chambers of the court, it should refer the case to the two general assemblies of civil, commercial and penal matters which is composed of twenty-two members. The decision then is rendered by a majority of fourteen judges.

In the Court of Cassation, the party must be represented by a lawyer registered in a list at the Bar for lawyers admitted before of the Court of Cassation.

The Court of Cassation has its own prosecution department, headed by a procurator general. The prosecution department must submit its written opinion in each case or demand before the Court of Cassation. This opinion usually has an influence on the decision of the court.

The Court of Cassation decisions are published in full text in a regular, systematic and well-indexed form in a magazine issued every three months by the court.

24. Economic Courts Law No. 120/2008 has established a new system of specialized Courts called Economic Courts. There is an Economic Court within the area of jurisdiction of each Court of Appeal. It is composed of first and appellate chambers. Each chamber of Economic Courts, whether preliminary or appeal, is composed of three judges. Preliminary chambers have jurisdiction of economic cases whose value does not exceed EGP 5 million (Article 6). Judgments of these chambers are appealable before Appellate chambers (Article 10). Appellate chambers have jurisdiction also as the first layer of jurisdiction, of economic cases whose value exceed EGP 5 million (Article 26). Judgments in these cases may be challenged before the Court of Cassation (Article 11).

§2. Members of the Judiciary

25. The courts operate with professional judges.

Members of the judiciary may be either justices of the bench or members of the prosecution department. Justices of the bench enjoy the greatest guarantee of independence, but members of the prosecution department are under the hierarchical authority of the Minister of Justice. In spite of this difference, all the members of the judiciary have the same status, and a magistrate may pass in the course of his career from the floor to the bench and conversely. They are recruited, and their careers unfold in the same way.

The status of magistrates is determined by Law No. 1972 called 'Law of the Judicial Authority, amended by Law No. 142/2006'. The Egyptian Constitution of 2014 contains some principles on judicial authority in Articles 184–195.

I. Appointment of Magistrates

26. Magistrates are appointed in Egypt by a Presidential Decree (Article 44 L.J.Auth.) upon the proposition of the Minister of Justice, after an appraisal of their worth by a committee presided by the President of the Court of Cassation.

The magistrates chosen by this committee are recruited as assistants in the prosecution department. In this department, they pass from one position to another until they reach the age of 30. Some of them are chosen then to be justices of the bench by the Supreme Council of Justice.

27. After their nomination either as members of the prosecution department or as justices of the bench, they are trained at the 'National Institution of Magistrates'. This institution is a public training centre for magistrates under the direct authority of the Minister of Justice.

The training at this institution is not a prerequisite for the recruitment of magistrates. It is offered to them after their appointment.

The training lasts three or six months. It consists of lectures in law and practical training in treating cases and in drafting decisions.

28. Access to the judicial body is also possible through the direct integration of professionals, either professors of law or attorneys at law, who have exercised their profession for a certain length of time. The law requires that a certain number of posts be filled through direct recruitment from lawyers as a percentage of the vacancies for a given year (Article 47 L.J.Auth.).

A magistrate appointed to his first post takes the following oath: 'I swear on the name of God to judge justly and to respect the laws.'

II. Career of Magistrates

29. The system of promotion of a magistrate during his career has a direct effect on his independence. If his promotion depends on the arbitrary power of the executive, the judge will be subject to pressure, and this will affect his independence.

Therefore, Egyptian law has adopted objective rules to govern the promotion of magistrates, under the control of the S.C.J.

The most important of these rules are the following:

(1) The promotion is made by a Presidential Decree after the approval of the S.C.J. (Article 44 L.J.Auth.).
(2) Promotion is subject to two conditions: fulfilling a certain number of years in the present rank and being capable of the higher rank.
(3) When the promotion commission proposes the promotion list, the Minister of Justice has to notify the magistrate, whose name is not included in the list, indicating the reasons for the absence of his name. The magistrate has the right to oppose that proposal, and his opposition has to be taken into consideration and decided upon before the issue of the promotion list. The appointment of the members of the Court of Cassation, the Presidents, Vice-Presidents and members of the courts of appeal, the Presidents and judges of the Tribunals of Grand Instance is made upon the approval of the S.C.M. (Article 44 L.J.Auth.).

III. Discipline

30. Magistrates, whether belonging to the bench or to the floor, can incur disciplinary sanctions if they commit disciplinary misdemeanours.

A disciplinary misdemeanour may not arise from an error in judgment. Disciplinary misconduct arises when a judge does not abide by the rules of his status or when his behaviour in his private life may jeopardize the honourable character of his function.

Disciplinary sanctions are limited only to censure or removal (Article 108 L.J.Auth.).

31. For judges in the Tribunals of Grand Instance, the censure may be taken by the President of the court to which the judge belongs, by the general assembly of the court, or by the Minister of Justice (Article 94 L.J.Auth.).

The disciplinary action is taken before a special council composed of, the most senior Presidents of courts of appeal who are not members of the S.C.J. as President, the two most senior judges of the Court of Cassation, and the two senior Vice-Presidents of the courts of appeal (Article 98 L.J.Auth. Amended by Law No. 142/2006).

The public prosecutor is the only one who may raise the disciplinary action. He raises it ex officio or at the request of the Minister of Justice or of the President of the court to which the judge belongs (Article 99 L.J.Auth. Amended by Law No. 142/2006).

The disciplinary action comes to an end by the dismissal or the retirement of the judge concerned.

Debates before the disciplinary council are adversary but secret. The council's decision has a judicial character, reasons must be given, and it is res judicata. The decision is final and may be attacked by the public prosecutor or by the condemned judge (Article 107 L.J.Auth. Amended by Law No. 142/2006).

IV. Incompatibilities

32. The function of magistrate is incompatible with the following:

(1) The exercise of commerce or of any other public or private function or profession (Article 72/1 L.J.Auth.).
(2) The exercise of any work, salaried or not, which affects his independence or harms the dignity of his function (Article 72/2 L.J.Auth.).
(3) To be an arbitrator, with or without fees, except if he is an arbitrator chosen by a party who is his relative from the fourth degree, or if he has been nominated as an arbitrator of the government or of a public authority. In both cases, he should obtain the approval of the S.C.M. (Article 63 L.J.Auth.).
(4) To represent a party before any court, or to write a legal opinion in his favour (Article 81 C.C.Pr.).
(5) To exercise politics or to belong to any political party. If a judge wants to contest in a parliamentary election, he should resign (Article 73 L.J.Auth.).

Chapter 2. The Legal Profession

§1. Exercise of the Legal Profession

I. Conditions for Admission

33. Egyptian law does not distinguish between an 'avocat' and an 'avoue', nor between a 'barrister' and a 'solicitor'. Egyptian lawyers exercise all the functions performed by either barristers or solicitors.

A lawyer who exercises the legal profession in Egypt has to belong to the Egyptian Bar. No one may exercise the functions of a lawyer if he is not a member of the Bar (Article 2 L. Law of Lawyers).

34. The organization of the Bar is governed by Law No. 17/1983, amended by Law No. 197/2008. According to this law, lawyers have the monopoly of representing the parties in courts and of giving regular legal advice (Article 3 Law of Lawyers).

Lawyers may exercise their profession either individually or as partners. A lawyer may also be a salaried employee of another lawyer or in a firm.

The legal profession in Egypt is open only to Egyptian citizens, but the minister of justice may permit to a foreigner lawyer to exercise advocacy in a certain case or in a certain subject, on the condition of reciprocity (Article 3/1 Law of Lawyers).

To be admitted to the Bar, one has to obtain a 'license' in law from an Egyptian university or from an equivalent foreign university.

35. A lawyer has to pass two years' training in the office of a lawyer practising before the Court of Cassation, or before Courts of Appeal. During these two years, the trainee attends lectures offered at the Bar by senior lawyers, professors of law and magistrates.

At the end of this training, he may be accepted as a lawyer before tribunals of first grade (Article 31 Law of Lawyers). After practising as a lawyer before these tribunals for five years, he may be admitted as a lawyer before Courts of Appeal (Article 35 Law of Lawyers). After ten years before these courts, he may be admitted as a lawyer before the Court of Cassation (Article 39 Law of Lawyers).

When a lawyer is admitted to practise before a higher court, he may also practise before lower tribunals.

§2. Rights and Duties

36. In the courthouse, lawyers wear a black gown with a cloak in white fur. The lawyer must abide by certain moral duties and a certain etiquette. To be able to exercise his functions, the lawyer is granted some immunities. His office is inviolable; it may not be searched except by a magistrate of the floor (Article 51 Law of Lawyers). A notice of any questioning of a lawyer in a crime should be sent to the President of the Bar who has the right to attend the procedures.

No court may ask a lawyer to act as a witness on facts he has known in the course of the exercise of his profession (Article 65 Law of Lawyers).

37. The profession of lawyer is incompatible with the exercise of commerce, public or private employment, and with being a minister or Speaker of the parliament.

38. Fees are freely agreed between the attorney and his client (Article 82 Law of Lawyers). They can be the subject of a written contract. The law gives directions for determining the amount of fees, in cases where there is no written agreement and a dispute arises about it. According to Article 82 (Law of Lawyers), it should be estimated taking into consideration the importance of the case, the efforts of the lawyer, the result he has obtained (the outcome of the case) and the grade of the lawyer.

In all cases, a quota limits agreement is forbidden (Article 82 Law of Lawyers).

If there is an amicable settlement of the case, the lawyer is entitled, nevertheless, to his fees (Article 83 Law of Lawyers).

§3. Discipline

39. Breaches by lawyers of laws, decrees, internal rules of the Bar may be the object of disciplinary proceedings. The disciplinary council for the lawyers is composed of the President of the Cairo Court of Appeal (as President of the council), two of its counsellors, two members of the council of the Bar, one of them chosen by the council and the other by the lawyer subject to the disciplinary proceedings (Article 107 Law of Lawyers). The proceedings are secret but adversary.

Appeal of the decision of the disciplinary council may be brought, within fifteen days, either by the lawyer concerned or by the prosecutor general. The appeal is decided by a counsel composed of four counsellors of the Court of Cassation, and three members of the council of the Bar. One of them is the President of the Bar or its Vice-President (Article 116 Law of Lawyers).

The sanctions incurred are censure, barring from the profession for a period not exceeding three years or disbarring (Article 98 Law of Lawyers). The council of the Bar may decide the temporary suspension of the lawyer's practise of the profession (Article 99 Law of Lawyers).

In case of a lawyer's misconduct at hearings, the court has to refer the matter to the procurator general who may bring it before the disciplinary council or before a criminal court. The victim of the misconduct of the lawyer is forbidden from participating in the trial (Article 50/2 Law of Lawyers).

§4. The Bar

40. In Egypt, there is only one Bar situated in Cairo with branches at the site of every Tribunal of Grand Instance (Article 144 Law of Lawyers). The Bar is a professional independent public institution with a public purpose. It is a juristic person. It has the power of organization, administration and discipline of the profession (Articles 120–121).

A council administers the Bar. It is presided by the President of the Bar. The members of the council of the Bar include representatives of the branches of the Bar and fifteen Lawyers of appeal elected by the general assembly of the Bar (Article 131 Law of Lawyers amended by Law No. 197/2008). All the lawyers, except trainees and retired lawyers, elect the members for four years (Articles 124–136 Law of Lawyers).

The council of the Bar decides, among other things, on the internal rules. It controls the finances of the Bar, manages its property and prepares its annual budget, and organizes the general services provided to lawyers (Article 143 Law of Lawyers).

The President of the Bar represents the Bar in civil life and in courts.

Chapter 3. Officials of the Courts

41. All officials of the courts in Egypt are public officers. The most important of them are the clerks and the bailiffs. The clerks and bailiffs are subject to laws and decrees governing all public officers in Egypt (Article 136 L.J.Auth.) and to rules disposed of by the Law of Judicial Authority (Articles 137–170).

§1. Clerks

42. According to Article 135/1 (L.J.Auth.), there should be a chief clerk and clerks in the Court of Cassation and in each Court of Appeal and Tribunal of Grand Instance. There are clerks also in every Tribunal of Small Instance presided by the chief clerk of the Tribunal of Grand Instance.

43. The clerk exercises two distinctive functions:

(1) He is a necessary element for the formation of the chamber in the hearing of the case. His presence in the court's session and in all proceedings held before the judge at a place other than the courtroom is necessary for its validity. He writes minutes about what happens in the session and signs the record of these minutes. He also signs the original copy of the judgment.
(2) He receives the petitions and requests, estimates the judicial expenses and collects them, and gives copies of the judgments of the orders upon request, or the records.

44. To be appointed as a clerk, one must be Egyptian and have a high school diploma or be a Bachelor of Law (Articles 137 and 138 L.J.Auth.).

If he is not a Bachelor of Law, he is appointed after passing an oral and written exam (Article 141 L.J.Auth.).

§2. Bailiffs

45. According to Article 135/2 (L.J.Auth.), there should be a chief bailiff and bailiffs in each Tribunal of Grand Instance. There are also bailiffs in every Tribunal of Small Instance presided over by the chief bailiff of the Grand Instance.

46. The bailiff exercise two distinctive functions:

(1) The notification of papers or documents which must be delivered to the adversary party (Article 6 C.C.Pr.).
(2) The enforcement of judgments and other enforceable instruments. He performs the seizure of movable material properties possessed by the debtor, either for security or execution (Article 6 and Article 279 C.C.Proc.). When he performs the seizure, he has the authority to collect the debt of the creditor

who requested the seizure. He also sells the properties seized in the public auction and collects the price. He establishes records to state the facts and the obstacles which he faces during his work. He assists the judge of execution in selling the real properties.

When the bailiff performs the seizure, he is called by Law No. 76/2007 'Execution officer'.

47. To be appointed as a bailiff, one must be Egyptian and have a high school diploma or be a Bachelor of Law (Article 148 L.J.Auth.).

He has to pass oral and written exams unless he is a Bachelor of Law (Article 149, Article 152 L.J.Auth.).

48. In performing his tasks, the bailiff acts as a representative of the state. He does not represent the creditor and does not act on his behalf. Therefore, he is obliged to act according to laws, decrees and directives of the judge under whose supervision and control he falls, and not according to directives of the party who requested his service.

Part II. Jurisdiction

Chapter 1. Domestic Jurisdiction

§1. Subject Matter Jurisdiction

I. Tribunal of Grand Instance (*Mahkama Kulia*)

49. The Tribunal of Grand Instance is the ordinary court of jurisdiction. It has jurisdiction to hear all cases not ascribed by the law to another court (Article 47/1 C.C.Pr.). It is the basic trial court in Egypt. Its jurisdiction is general covering every case not specifically assigned to other tribunals.

Apart from this general jurisdiction, the Tribunal of Grand Instance has exclusive jurisdiction for certain types of dispute whatever the value of the claim. Examples of this exclusive jurisdiction of the Tribunal of Grand Instance are: bankruptcy and cases concerning patent law.

The President of the Tribunal of Grand Instance has jurisdiction of his own for orders upon requests (Article 27 C.C.Proc.).

II. Tribunal of Small Instance (*Mahkama Guzeea*)

50. The Tribunal of Small Instance hears all cases involving personal or property claims not exceeding the value of EGP 40,000 (EGP 5,000 for final judgment).

In some cases, the Tribunal of Small Instances has exclusive jurisdiction for certain types of disputes, whatever the value of the claim. Examples: disputes concerning the use of irrigation water, the cleaning of canals, the fixation of the borders between real estates, the evaluation of the distance to be left between real estates or buildings, division of property between co-owners, salaries and wages, relations between landlords and tenants.

III. Jurisdiction for Urgent Cases

51. According to Article 45/2 C.C.Proc., the jurisdiction for urgent cases is determined as follows:

(1) The Tribunal for Urgent Matters. This tribunal is a specialized court, which deals only with urgent cases. It has jurisdiction for all urgent cases raised in

the city where it operates. There is a Tribunal for Urgent Matters in each city where there is a Tribunal of Grand Instance.

(2) The Tribunal of Small Instance, which exists in the city where there is no Tribunal for Urgent Matters, has jurisdiction for urgent cases.

(3) If the urgent case is raised as an ancillary claim procedure in a substantial case, the tribunal competent of this case has also jurisdiction for the urgent case. The plaintiff has the choice to raise the case either before the tribunal mentioned above in points (1) and (2) or before the tribunal competent of the substantial case.

52. Subject matter jurisdiction of Economic Courts.

According to Article 6 of Law No. 120/2008, Economic Courts have exclusive jurisdiction to hear the disputes and legal actions arising from the following Laws:

(1) The Law Regulating the Companies Receiving and Investing Assets.
(2) The Capital Market Law.
(3) The Investment Guarantee and Incentive Law.
(4) The Lease Finance Law.
(5) The Law Protecting the National Economy from the Effects resulting from Harmful Practice in International Trade.
(6) The matters regulating transfer of technology, commercial agencies, bank operations, bankruptcy and composition with creditors under the Commercial Code.
(7) The Real Estate Financing Law.
(8) The Intellectual Property Right Protection Law.
(9) The Telecommunication Regulation Law.
(10) The Electronic Signature and the Establishment of the Information Technology Development Authority Law.
(11) The Competition Protection and Anti-Monopolistic Practices Law.
(12) The Joint Stock, Limited Partnership by Shares and Limited Liability Companies.
(13) The Central Bank, Bank Establishment and Currency Law.

They have no jurisdiction to hear any other economic dispute arising from the application of any other law.

The limited jurisdiction of Economic Courts is critical. The Law attempts to capture all aspects of economic activities, but this limitation draws a distinction between two groups of disputes having the same nature and importance.

§2. Territorial Jurisdiction (Venue)

53. The basic rule of territorial jurisdiction is that the plaintiff must summon the defendant before the court of the defendant's domicile at the date when the action is brought (Article 49/1 C.C.Proc.).

According to Egyptian law, the domicile is the place where the person usually resides (Article 40 Civ.C.).

If the defendant has more than one domicile, the plaintiff may choose any of the courts of the defendant's domiciles. If the defendant has no domicile in Egypt, he may be summoned before the court of his residence. If the defendant has neither a domicile nor a residence in Egypt, the plaintiff may refer the matter to the court of his domicile, or of his residence. If the plaintiff has neither a domicile in Egypt nor a residence, the jurisdiction would be for the court of Cairo (Article 61 C.C.Pr).

If the defendant is a juristic person, the jurisdiction will be for the court of his registered office (Article 52 C.C.Proc.). If the juristic person has branches, and the case concerns a certain branch, the jurisdiction is for the court of the place where the branch exists (Article 52/2 C.C.Proc.).

In case of several defendants, if the object of the claims against them are the same or connected, the plaintiff may refer the matter, at his choice, to the court of domicile of one of them (Article 49/3 C.C.Proc.), but if it appears from the circumstances that the case has been brought to a certain court in order to force one of the defendants into a court other than his domicile's court, the court shall decline to entertain it.

54. Exceptions to the rule. The rule 'actor sequitur forum rei' has some exceptions, where the law finds another court more suitable to deal with the case. The most important exceptions, in Egyptian law, are the following.

55. For real property actions, the court which has jurisdiction is that where the property or part of it is located. The same rule applies to actions concerning possession of real estate. If a case concerns more than one parcel of real property, the action may be brought in any place where any of the properties is located. This exception applies only to the action which has as its object real property or a possession of it; it does not apply in matters of leases for rent and rural leases (Article 50 C.Civ.Proc.).

56. The actions raised from corporation and private associations, foundations and establishments against their partners or members concerning the affairs of those institutions, should be raised before the court where the juristic person has its registered office. The same rule applies for actions raised from a partner or a member against another partner or member (Article 52 C.C.Proc.).

57. In matters of succession of property, the court, which has jurisdiction before the division of the property, is the court within whose territorial jurisdiction the deceased had his last domicile. This exception includes only claims raised by heirs against heirs and claims raised by creditors against heirs (Article 53 C.C.Proc.).

58. The claim of bankruptcy of a merchant has to be raised before the court where his place of business exists.

59. Particular options open to the plaintiff. For some actions, the law gives the plaintiff the choice to choose between two or several courts. The most important are the followings examples:

(1) In commercial actions based upon a contract, the plaintiff may refer the matter either to the court of the defendant's domicile or to the court where the contract has been concluded and totally or partially executed or to the court where the contract has to be executed (Article 55 C.C.Proc.).
(2) In matters of alimony, the jurisdiction is for either the court of the plaintiff's or the defendant's domicile (Article 57 C.C.Proc.).
(3) For actions arising from a legal act in which both a property right or the defendant's right in rem and right in personam are at stake, the plaintiff may refer the matter either to the court of the defendant's domicile or to the court where the realty is located (Article 50/2 C.C.Proc.). These actions are called mixed actions, for example, the action for the validity and efficacy of a contract conveying real property.
(4) Claims for amounts for rent of residences, or actions from contractors and suppliers may be filed in the court of the defendant's domicile or in that of the plaintiff's domicile if the agreement has been concluded or executed where the domicile is located (Article 56 C.C.Proc.).
(5) Insurance claims may be brought before the court of the insured person's domicile (the plaintiff) or to the court of the defendant's registered office. If the insurance contract concerns property, the action may be brought before the court of the place where such property is located (Article 58 C.C.Proc.).

§3. Adjustments of Jurisdiction Rules

60. The court jurisdiction extends to the hearing of defences. This is the implementation of the traditional principle according to which 'the judge of the action is the judge of the exception'. This extension of the jurisdiction concerns any defence presented by the defendant, whether on merits or procedural.

Sometimes, the exception contains a defence that, in fact, is a preliminary issue of which the decision is necessary for the judgment of the main action. In this case, if the preliminary issue does not fall within the jurisdiction of the court examining the main action, this court must stay the judgment until the court which has exclusive jurisdiction of that issue rules on it.

61. The most common preliminary issues which do not fall within the jurisdiction of the court examining the main action are the following:

(1) If the main action is of the jurisdiction of the Tribunal of First Instance, and the preliminary issue is of the jurisdiction of the Tribunal of Grand Instance.
(2) If the preliminary issue is the legality of an administrative act; this legality is of the exclusive jurisdiction of the administrative court (Council of State).
(3) If the preliminary issue is the constitutionality of a law or a decree, this matter is of the exclusive jurisdiction of the Constitutional Court.

62. As for ancillary claims, the Tribunal of Grand Instance has jurisdiction to hear all ancillary claims as long as they do not fall within the exclusive jurisdiction of a criminal court, an administrative court or the Constitutional Court.

The Tribunals of Small Instance may hear ancillary claims only if the latter fall within their subject matter jurisdiction (Article 46 C.C.Pr.).

63. Because the venue is not determined by consideration of public policy, the parties may agree to give territorial jurisdiction to a tribunal, which does not have the jurisdiction according to the rules of law. This agreement is valid either before the filing of the claim or before the hearings. However, it may not be concluded before the beginning of the judicial process, if the agreement is contrary to a territorial jurisdiction which is an exception to the rule 'actor sequitur forum rei' (Article 62/2 C.C.Proc.).

When the agreement is valid, the plaintiff has the option to raise his action either before the tribunal of the defendant's domicile or before the tribunal agreed upon its jurisdiction (Article 61/1 C.C.Proc.). Such a court cannot decline to proceed.

64. On the contrary, because the subject matter jurisdiction is determined by considerations of public order, the parties are not allowed to change it, by agreement. Such an agreement is void and has no legal effect.

§4. Resolution of Jurisdiction Conflicts

65. Territorial jurisdiction has to be disclaimed by the defendant. This disclaiming should be put forward '*in limine litis*' before any claim, defence or demeurer of non-admissibility. All reasons for disclaiming have to be raised together (Article 108 C.C.Proc.).

The court may not declare territorial non-jurisdiction by itself.

Subject matter non-jurisdiction is of public order. Every party, whether plaintiff or defendant may disclaim the subject matter jurisdiction at any stage of the process even after submitting his claims or defences (Article 109 C.C.Pro.).

66. When the court declares that it exercises no jurisdiction, it states which court has jurisdiction, except when the court is a criminal court, an administrative court or a foreign court. Then it must transfer the case to the designated competent court. The proceedings are not interrupted, and the plaintiff does not have to start them from the beginning in the new court. The designated court is obliged to jurisdiction stated by the first court (Article 110 C.Civ.Proc.). If the decision of non-jurisdiction has been appealed, the proceeding in the court to which the case has been transferred stops till the decision of non-jurisdiction is final (Article 212 C.Civ.Proc.).

67. When the court declares that it exercises jurisdiction, it has the choice either to rule only on the jurisdiction or to rule also on the merits.

When the first instance court declares that it exercises no jurisdiction and transfers the case to the court that has jurisdiction, this decision may be challenged by an ordinary appeal (Article 212 C.Civ.Proc.). If the Court of Appeal rules that the court to which the case had been transferred exercises jurisdiction, the court's office transfers the case back to that court. If the Court of Appeal rules that the initial court which declares non-jurisdiction has jurisdiction, it quashes its decision and transfers the case to it.

When the court declares that it exercises jurisdiction and has ruled on the merits in the same judgment, this judgment may be challenged by an ordinary appeal, on both jurisdiction and merits. When the Court of Appeal rules that the Court of First Instance did not have proper jurisdiction, the Court of Appeal may not rule on the merits, it should transfer the case to the Tribunal of First Instance it deems to have jurisdiction.

Chapter 2. International Jurisdiction

§1. Rules Applicable in the Absence of a Treaty

68. The Code of Civil Procedure in Egypt deals with international jurisdiction of Egyptian courts in Articles 28–35. This jurisdiction arises when the dispute presents a foreign element. This element may concern the nature of the parties (nationality, domicile) or the subject matter of the dispute (location of property, place where a contract was signed or a legal act took place).

I. Privilege of Jurisdiction for Egyptian Nationals in Egyptian Courts

69. According to Article 28 of the Code of Civil Procedure, the Egyptian courts have jurisdiction of claims against Egyptian citizens even if they have no domicile or residence in Egypt.

This general rule which gives privilege to Egyptian nationals applies only when the defendant is Egyptian. It does not apply when he is the plaintiff.

On the other hand, this rule does not apply to property action concerning property located in a foreign country (Article 28 C.C.Proc.)

Article 28 of the Code of Civil Procedure applies the same rule, and its exceptions, to cases raised against foreigners who have a domicile or a residence in Egypt.

II. Jurisdiction for Claims Against a Foreigner Who Has No Domicile or Residence in Egypt

70. Article 30, Code of Civil Procedure, enumerates the cases in which the Egyptian courts have jurisdiction for claims raised against a foreigner who has neither domicile nor residence in Egypt.

71. The most important are the following:

(1) If the foreigner has elected domicile in Egypt for the execution of a legal act.
(2) If the case concerns a property located in Egypt or concerning an obligation started, executed or has to be executed in Egypt, or concerning a bankruptcy registered in Egypt.
(3) If the case is an opposition to a contact of marriage to be concluded before an Egyptian notary.
(4) If the claim concerns the resolution of a marriage, a divorce, or separation of a couple, and the claim was raised by a wife who has lost her nationality by marriage while she had a domicile in Egypt or raised by a wife who has a domicile in Egypt, against her husband who had a domicile in Egypt, if the husband has abandoned his wife and took up domicile abroad after the resolution of the marriage, the divorce or the separation, or if the husband has been evicted out of Egypt.

(5) If the claim is concerning the paternity of a child or his custody and the child has a residence in Egypt.
(6) If the claim is a non-patrimonial action, and the plaintiff is an Egyptian or a foreigner who has a domicile in Egypt, while the defendant has unknown domicile abroad or Egyptian law is applicable in the case.
(7) If one of the defendants has a domicile or a residence in Egypt.

III. Jurisdiction for Successions

72. Article 31 (C.C.Proc.) declares the jurisdiction of Egyptian courts of all matters and claims concerning successions, if the deceased had his last domicile in Egypt or the deceased was Egyptian or if all his property, or part of it, has been in Egypt.

IV. Extension of International Jurisdiction

73. According to Article 32 (C.C.Proc.), in cases in which the Egyptian courts have no jurisdiction, they will have jurisdiction if the defendant accepts this expressly or tacitly. A clause attributing jurisdiction in international relations, according to Egyptian law is valid.

74. On the other hand, if a case is in the jurisdiction of an Egyptian court, this court will have jurisdiction of all ancillary claims and preliminary issues (Article 33 C.C.Proc.).

75. Egyptian courts also have jurisdiction of all provisional and protective measures out of urgency even if they exercise no jurisdiction to rule on the merits (Article 34 C.C.Proc.).

V. Domestic Rules of Territorial Jurisdiction Applied to International Disputes

76. International jurisdiction is governed by the domestic rules of territorial jurisdiction. As we have mentioned before, if the defendant has no known domicile or residence in Egypt, the plaintiff may refer the action to the court of his domicile, or if he has no domicile in Egypt, to the court of his residence. If the plaintiff has neither a domicile nor a residence in Egypt, the territorial jurisdiction would be for the Court of Cairo (Article 61 C.C.Proc.). In this case, the plaintiff may choose any court of the courts of Cairo.

VI. Resolution of Jurisdictional Conflicts

77. The resolution of jurisdictional conflicts concerning international disputes falls under the same rules as those concerning domestic conflicts.

The court does not declare, by itself, that it has no jurisdiction except in case the defendant was absent. If the defendant did not appear before the court, in cases of which the court has no jurisdiction, the court declares, ex officio, that it has no jurisdiction (Article 35 C.Civ.Proc.). If the defendant attends the procedures at an audience or submits his defence to the court, he is considered to have accepted the court's jurisdiction (Article 32 C.Civ.Proc.).

If the court declares that it exercises no jurisdiction, it does not have to designate the foreign court exercising jurisdiction and transfer the case to it. It simply declares that it has no jurisdiction.

§2. International Treaties

78. The rules that have been discussed, which are contained in the Code of Civil Procedure, may be replaced by rules contained in international treaties. Such treaties, when approved by the legislator, are considered part of Egyptian law. These treaties may be bilaterally concluded by two countries, or multilateral concluded by a group of countries, such as the international convention concerning the unification of some rules concerning the civil competence in case of maritime accidents concluded in Brussels on 10 May 1952 and to which Egypt has joined on 10 March 1955, or the convention concerning the settlement of disputes about investments between the Arab States in which the investments are located, and the citizens of the other countries concluded on 10 June 1974 and joined by Egypt on 22 October 1974.

On the other hand, these treaties could deal with particular matters such as copyright, development and investment, international transport, or with the entire matter of jurisdiction.

VI. Resolution of Jurisdictional Conflicts

[illegible]

Part III. Actions, Claims and Defences

Chapter 1. The Judicial Action

§1. Definition

79. The Code of Civil Procedure did not provide a definition for judicial action. Egyptian authors have different definitions of the term.

In my opinion, the action is a right for the plaintiff to obtain a decision on his claim in his favour, that is a decision stating that his claim is well-founded.

The action is a right in itself other than the substantive right. It is not just a right to lay a claim or a defence before a judge, but the right to obtain a remedy.

80. The right of action has to be distinguished from the right to lay a claim. A party may have the right to lay a claim, but not the right of action.

The right to lay a claim is distinguished from the claim itself, which is its embodiment before the court.

81. The claim has to be distinguished from the demand, which is the act of procedure by which the process starts before the court. It is the first act in the judicial process. The claim is the object of the demand or the object of the defence presented against the demand.

If the plaintiff has the right to lay a claim, his demand (or claim) is admissible, but this demand (or claim) may be refused on merits. To be accepted on merits, the plaintiff should have the right of action.

82. The right of raising a claim has to be distinguished from the right for anybody to have access to the courts, which is a public right to justice. The first right concerns a certain person or persons, aiming to obtain a certain judicial remedy. The second concerns everyone and consists of having access to courts in general.

83. One must notice the different meanings of the term action in the articles of the Egyptian Code of Civil Procedure and in judicial practice. The term action is used, in Egypt, in the meaning of right of action, right to lay a claim, the claim, the demand and the process.

§2. Conditions of the Right of Action

84. To have the right of action, in the sense of having the right to a favourable judgment, the following conditions are necessary:

(a) The existence of a substantive right or a legal position. As the action is a means to protect a right or a legal position, it presupposes the existence of a right or a position which is protected by law; 'where there is no right, there is no action'.
(b) The violation of this right or of a legal position. The right of action does not arise if the owner of the right or legal position has not been deprived of its benefits. Without this deprivation, no need would exist for judicial protection, and consequently, no interest in seeking judgment by demand. The right of action does not exist before the violation of a substantive right or of a legal position.
(c) The active standing to sue: which means the personality of the right of action. This standing arises for the owner of the substantive right or of the legal position against those responsible for the violation of that right (passive standing).

85. As an exception, the right of action may arise for someone who does not own the right protected by the action, as in the following cases:

(1) The General Procurator does not have a subject right, although he has the right of action, in civil and commercial matters in some cases. In these cases, he stands for the interest of law to protect the interests of society.
(2) A union has a right of action when the collective interest of the trade, or industry it represents, has been damaged (Article 16 Law No. 85/1942). The union has the right of action even if it does not represent all the workers in the section concerned.
(3) A union has a right of action if it is a part in a collective labour contract if the breach of this contract has damaged the interest of one of its members (Article 165 Law No. 12/2003).

This right of action for the unions is not granted to associations. The law does not recognize the right of action for the association to protect its objectives. Thus, the association against alcoholism has no right of action to prevent a hotel from offering alcohol to its clients.

§3. Admissibility of the Action (Interest in the Action)

86. According to Article 3 of the Code of Civil Procedure (amended by Law No. 81/96):

> Any action, demand or defence, is not admissible according to the rules of this law or any other law, unless the plaintiff has a personal, direct, present and legitimate interest.

> A probable interest is enough if the demand aims to take precaution against imminent harm or to save the means of evidence which might be demolished in case of litigation.
>
> The court has to announce the non-admissibility by itself, in any stage of the process.

According to Article 3*bis* of the Code of Civil Procedure (amended by Law No. 81/96):

> The rule of the previous article does not apply where law grants the general procurator the power to raise the action, to intervene in a case, or to challenge the judgment; nor in cases where the law grants the right to raise the action or the challenge or the petition to someone who has not a personal legitimate interest.

Thus, Article 3 states for an action to be admissible, a unique condition which is the existence of interest.

87. The capacity of the party is not a condition for the admissibility of action, but a condition for the validity of the procedural acts accomplished by the parties.

88. The interest is a condition in order that the court examines the claim contained in a demand, in a defence or in a challenge. It is a general condition for the admissibility of any act of procedure containing a desire submitted to the judge to take a decision on it.

It is not correct to understand the interest as a material or intangible advantage that the plaintiff (or the author of the act of procedure) hopes to gain. No sane person goes to the judge without hoping to gain an advantage.

The interest as a condition for admissibility should be understood as an application of the principle of the economy in the process. The court should not waste its time examining any demand (*late sensu*) of the party if it does not help in reaching the judicial protection of the right or legal position which this party is seeking to protect.

The sanction of the lack of interest is the inadmissibility of the demand (*in lato senso*).

89. The interest in the action does not exist if there is no need to examine the merits. This happens if the examining of the merits would not help in realizing the judicial protection which the plaintiff seeks. In other words, if any search on the merits would not change the result of the case. In this case, the plaintiff has no interest that the merits would be examined, and the court should announce the inadmissibility of his demand, for lack of interest.

90. As an application of this condition of interest, the action is not admissible in the following cases:

(a) If there is no rule of law upon which the demand of the plaintiff may be based. The action is not admissible if it seeks to protect a mere economic interest which is not protected by law (Cass.Civ. Chamber 5 November 1989 in Case No. 778/57), or to protect an immoral situation.
   Therefore, Article 3 (C.Civ.Proc.) implies that the interest should be legitimate.
(b) If it is obvious that the right of action did not yet exist, for instance, if the term to which the right of the plaintiff is suspended was not yet realized.
(c) If it is obvious that the right of action of the plaintiff has been prescribed, or has been stated by a previous judgment obtaining the 'res judicata'. To this, Article 3 (C.Civ.Proc.) refers when it implies that the interest should be present, and existing. If Article 3 allows, in some cases, actions when the interest is probable, it is more correct to say that in these cases, the interest is present but the violation to the plaintiff's right is probable 'in future'. In spite of the probability of the violation, the plaintiff has a present interest in his action.
(d) If the person who is raising the claim or the one against whom the claim is raised are not parties in the right of action, Article 3 (C.Civ.Proc.) refers to this when stating that the interest should be personal and direct. Therefore, a claim for the nullity of a contract is not admissible if it is raised by a person who is not a party of this contract.

§4. Vexation Litigation

91. In accordance with the general theory of misuse of a right, there can be a vexation of the right to raise a claim or to defend, or of the right to proceed by any act of procedure (Article 188/1 C.Civ.Proc.).

The vexation character is apparent when the party (plaintiff or defendant) acts out of malice or when he acts for the purpose of harming his adversary, for example, if he indulges in dilatory proceedings.

According to several articles in the Code of Civil Procedure, the party who proceeds in court in a vexation manner may be fined (Articles 14, 85, 110, 115, 159).

Chapter 2. Claims and Defences

§1. Claims

92. A claim may be either initial or incidental. The initiator's main claim is that by which a party takes the initiative of judicial proceedings by submitting his demands to the court. It institutes a suit.

In Egyptian law, the form of the initial claim is the same before all courts of civil jurisdiction. It is embodied in a petition deposited and registered in the court and then notified to the defendant by a bailiff (Articles 63, 230 and 243 C.Civ.Proc.).

93. A claim brought in the course of a suit is an incidental or ancillary claim. There are several kinds of ancillary claims: additional claim from the plaintiff, counter-claim from the defendant, and intervention from a stranger of the suit either voluntarily or forced by a request of the party or by the court itself. It results in the introduction of a third party in the suit.

An ancillary claim is only admissible insofar as it is related through a sufficient link to the main claim (Articles 124, 125, 126 C.Civ.Proc.).

94. The initial defendant can become a plaintiff through a counter-claim. This counter-claim is called the claim of the defendant.

§2. Defences

95. The word defence encompasses the different forms that can be taken by the defendant to have the demand of the plaintiff rebutted.

Defences are of three kinds: defence on merits, procedural exception and demurer.

I. Defence on Merits

96. A defence on merits consists of any means aiming to have the demand of the opposing party rejected as unjustified after examination of the merits.

The defence on merit is the demonstration that the right of action claimed by the opposing party is groundless in fact and/or in law. Its aim is to refuse the opposing party's claim. It may be brought at any level of proceedings, in first instance and in appeal.

II. Procedural Exceptions

97. A procedural exception consists of any means aimed at having the procedure declared irregular or extinct, at having its course suspended, or at having the court declared without jurisdiction of the action.

98. A procedural exception is directed against the procedures and not against the claim itself.

Procedural exceptions are not enumerated by the law exclusively. The law enumerates some of them, but any exception which has the aspects of a procedural exception is considered as such.

The most frequent exceptions are the following:

- Exception of non-jurisdiction (*exceptio declinatoria*).
- Exception of nullity (voidance).
- Exception of joinder of actions.
- Exception of suit pending elsewhere (*lis alibi pendens*).
- Dilatory plea.

99. To be admissible, procedural exceptions must be raised simultaneously, including all their reasons, before any defence on the merits or demurer (*in limine litis*), except if the rules referred to are of public interest (Article 108 C.Civ.Proc.).

If the procedural exception is accepted, this does not forbid the party from acting again by a correct procedure or before the court which has jurisdiction.

III. Demurers

100. A demurer consists of any means aiming to have the opposing party's demand, or defence declared inadmissible, without being examined on the merits. Demurers are of two kinds: demurers related to merits and demurers related to procedures. A demurer related to procedures is governed by the same rules as procedural exceptions.

101. A demurer related to the merits has a sole reason, which is the lack of interest in examining the merits, as mentioned above in detail.

A demurer related to merit is possible at any level of proceedings even on appeal (Article 115 C.Civ.Proc.).

It is treated, from this point, as a defence on merits. It must be put in by the court itself when it is relevant to public order. For example, the demurer for 'res judicata' (Article 116 C.Civ.Proc.).

Chapter 3. Sanctions on Procedural Irregularities

102. There are many kinds of sanctions for procedural irregularities. The most important are nullity of acts of procedure, and the fall of the procedural right.

§1. Nullity of Acts of Procedure

103. The Egyptian Code of Civil Procedure of 1968 has organized the rules of nullity of acts of procedure in Articles 20–24. It has adopted in full the ideas which were submitted by Prof. F. Waly in his thesis in 1958 (F. Waly, *Theory of Nullity of Acts of Procedure, A Thesis*, Cairo University, 1958. Two editions 1959, 1997).

According to these ideas, and to the articles of the Egyptian Code, the rules of the nullity of acts of procedure are the following.

I. Cases in Which the Nullification Is Granted

104. We must make a distinction between nullity due to a defect in form, and nullity due to a defect in the substantive element. (This distinction was adopted later by the New French Code of Civil Procedure, Articles 114–118.)

A. *Nullity Due to a Defect in Form*

105. This defect may result in the nullity of the act of procedure in two cases (Article 20 C.Civ.Proc.):

(1) If this sanction is provided expressly by a text of law. In this case, nullification will be granted by the judge unless the contravening party proves that the function of the form defected has been realized in spite of the defect.
(2) If the sanction is not provided expressly by a text of law. In this case, the judge will not grant the nullity of the act unless the requesting party proves that the defect of the act has caused the non-realization of the function of the defected form.

106. By this theory, the sanction may be applied whether there is a text of law expressly providing the sanction or not, whether the defected form is a substantive form in itself or not, and whether the form is of public interest or of private interest.

B. *Substantive Nullity*

107. The act of procedure is a legal act. It has substantive elements necessary for its validity. These elements include the authority of the acting person, his standing to act, his capacity and the subject matter of the act.

A defect of one of these elements results in the nullity of the act, whether there is an express text of law providing the sanction or not, and disregarding the realization of the function of the element defected. The sanction of nullity is applied de jure because of the defect.

II. Rules of Nullity

108. Nullities either for defects of form or for substantive defect, when existing, are governed by the same rules. These rules are only different depending on whether the formality or the substantive element defected is of public order or for a party's private interest. If the nullity is for a party's interest, the nullity may only be pronounced by the request of the party, in whose interest the defected formality or substantive element has been required by law. The court may not pronounce the nullity by itself (sua sponte). The other party may not request the nullity of the act defected even if the declaration of the nullity is in his interest.

This nullity of private interest has to be raised '*in limine litis*', it may not be raised if the requesting party has presented a defence on the merits or a demurer, or has previously presented other procedural exceptions.

This nullity disappears if the party waives his right of raising the nullity expressly or tacitly (Article 21 C.Civ.Proc.).

109. All these above-mentioned rules do not apply if the nullity is of public order. If so, the court may pronounce the nullity sua sponte at any time of the proceedings even in appeal or 'cassation'. Any party who has an interest in the nullity of the act may request this nullity. The party, who has renounced his right to request the nullity may, nevertheless, request it. The public prosecutor, if involved in the suit, may also request the nullity of any act of procedure as long as the nullity is of public interest.

For an example of a formality of a public order nature, the signature of a lawyer admitted at courts of appeal on the petition of appeal. As an example of a substantive element of a public order nature, the capacity of the party.

§2. Lapse of the Procedural Right

110. The right of acting in the suit may be bound by a time limit within which it should be exercised.

Non-compliance with the time limit results in the loss of the right to act. The sanction is the lapse of the procedural right. If the party acts after the expiration of the time imposed, he thus acts without any right to act. His act is void. In this case, two sanctions apply: the lapse of this right to act and the nullity of his act.

The sanction of the lapse is applied strictly. It applies regardless of the realization or not of the function of the time imposed.

Possible attenuation of the sanction in matters of nullity of form may not be applied.

Part IV. Proceedings

Chapter 1. Conciliation Before Trial

111. Egyptian law does not confer to judges the mission to conciliate the parties, but, the parties may, after the initiation of the lawsuit, reach a settlement. They present it to the court which states it in the hearing record, and thus has the power of an enforceable instrument (Article 103 C.Civ.Proc.).

112. Recently, Law No. 7 of the year 2000 has established a special system of conciliation. This Law has been amended by Law No. 6/2017. This new system applies only for litigations between a public entity and a private person, by the exception of litigations concerning the Ministry of Defence or of artillery production and litigations concerning real estates and some other litigations mentioned in Article 4 of Law No. 7/2000. Law No. 72/2017 (Investment Law) added another exception, in Article 5, which is 'all disputes arising of the application of this law'.

113. According to Law No. 7/2002 (as amended), the litigation has to be submitted to a special committee composed of a retired judge as President and two members representing the two parties. If necessary, it can be chosen from present judges or from retired members of judicial organizations (Article 2/2 and Article 3/1 of Law No. 6/2017).

The committee hears the two parties who have the right to submit their arguments and documents.

If the plaintiff goes to the court before submitting his claim to this committee, his action will be deemed inadmissible (Article 11 Law No. 7/2000).

114. The committee announces its decision on the case within thirty days, starting from the submission of the demand to it. It should reason for its decision.

If the parties do not accept this decision within fifteen days, or if thirty days expire without declaring the opinion of the committee, each party may raise his lawsuit to the court (Article 10 of Law No. 7/2000).

The decision should be delivered to the private party and the competent public authority within seven days. If the decision is accepted within fifteen days of that delivery, the committee states this agreement in a record signed by the parties and joins to the hearing record of the committee and will have the power of an enforceable instrument (Law No. 6/2017) and the decision will be notified to the public authority for execution.

According to Article 3 Law No. 7/2000 amended by Law No. 6/2017, even if the administrative authority does not approve the decision of the committee, it will be enforceable towards it, if the value of the litigation does not exceed EGP 40,000 or if the litigation concerns financial rights due to employees of the administrative party. In this case, the decision may be challenged before the judicial competent court. This challenge does not stay its enforcement unless the court decides so.

115. According to Article 8 of Law No. 120/2008 concerning Economic Courts, a preparation panel prepares the cases. This panel shall exert effort to propose a settlement between the parties. If the parties agree, minutes of this settlement shall be signed by the parties and adjoined to the minutes before the court. The case shall be, consequently, terminated, and the minutes stating the settlement will have the force of the enforceable instrument.

116. According to Articles 85–87 and 88–89 of Law No. 72/2017 (Investment Law), all disputes or demands arising out of contracts of investments are to be submitted to a special committee inside the concerned ministry or the council of ministers. The decisions of these committees are binding, but the investor may challenge the decision or raise his case to the competent judicial or Arbitral Tribunal.

Chapter 2. Proceedings in First Instance

§1. PRINCIPLES GOVERNING A LAWSUIT

117. There are some principles that govern the Egyptian lawsuit in all courts.

I. Principle of the Demand

118. The first principle is the principle of demand. No lawsuit starts without the initiation of a party. The judge may not act without demand.

The demand is necessary not only to start the lawsuit but also to start any judicial process to challenge the sentence, such as the process of appeal or 'cassation'.

This principle also applies for the continuation of the judicial process if the plaintiff renounces his demand; the judge may not continue to examine it.

119. The judge is bound by the demands of the parties. He is bound by all the elements of the demand: parties, object and cause. He may not judge against or in favour of a person who is not a party in the demand. He may not decide issues beyond or different from what is claimed, and he must decide on everything that is claimed.

If the plaintiff asks a certain amount of money in a damage case and the expert's report states that the plaintiff is entitled to more than what he asked, the court may not grant it, sua sponte, to the plaintiff. If the plaintiff asks for the validity and efficacy of a contract of sale of a real estate, the court may not add to its judgment the ejection of the defendant from the real estate.

The judge is also bound by the cause of the demand; he may not judge for a cause different than that which has been submitted as the cause of the demand.

II. Principle of Adversary Proceedings

120. The lawsuit is governed by the principle of adversary proceedings, with the following results:

(1) No party may be judged without being heard. Each party must be given the opportunity to submit his defence to the court. The principle is deemed respected whether the adversary has submitted his defence or not as far as he has been validly summoned and given the opportunity to defend.
(2) The parties must inform each other of the facts upon which their demands are founded and of the documents and papers submitted to the court.
(3) The judge may not base his sentence upon his personnel knowledge of the facts, he must rely only upon facts brought by the party and of which the other party has been informed.

§2. Ordinary Proceedings

121. Ordinary proceedings have to be followed in ordinary courts, whether Tribunals of Great Instance or of Small Instance. The same proceedings have to be followed either in a Court of First Instance or in a Court of Appeal, and whether the suit is urgent or concerning the merits.

I. Introduction of the Instance

122. The instance is introduced by a petition of the case filed by the plaintiff or his lawyer. The plaintiff may not assert at any time more distinct claims against the same defendant or defendants in a single lawsuit. This is not possible unless the claims are closely related as if all the claims have the same cause.

The petition is handed to the court clerk and registered on the roll.

The action is considered raised at the moment of its registration in the court. By this registration, the case is considered open.

Registration also has other consequences, among which are as follows:

(a) It determines the date from which interest begins to run.
(b) It prevents the plaintiff from bringing another action on the same claim.
(c) It determines the authority of the court.
(d) It prevents the plaintiff from adding to or changing the elements of his claim except in cases permitted by law.

The petition must contain the names, surnames, occupations and addresses of the parties and those of their representatives, date of the petition, name of the court where the action is brought, facts, demands of the plaintiff, grounds upon which they are founded (Article 63 C.Civ.Proc.) and the court before which the defendant has to appear. There is no requirement that the plaintiff specify the law relied upon.

If the plaintiff is domiciled outside the jurisdiction area of the court, he must indicate a domicile inside the jurisdictional area. If no domicile is so indicated, the defendant may notify him to the clerk's office in the court (Article 12 C.Civ.Proc.).

The petition must have a duplicate for the file, and a copy for each of the defendants (Article 65 C.Civ.Proc.) has to be signed by the plaintiff or his attorney.

123. When the petition is handed to the court clerk to be registered, the plaintiff has to attach to it the documents that serve as proof of his demand, a statement of his means of proof, a receipt that indicates that he has paid the procedure fees and an explanatory note or a statement that the petition does not need any explanation.

The clerk then fixes the date of the first audience and writes it on the copies of the summons of the petition. In fixing this date, the clerk should leave a certain period between the notification to the defendant to appear in court and the date of the first instance. This period is twenty-four hours in urgent cases, and from eight to fifteen days in the cases on merits according to the type of the court (Article 66 C.Civ.Proc.).

124. Within three days of the registration of the petition, the clerk should send a letter to the defendant informing him that the petition has been registered, indicating the name of the plaintiff, his claims and the date of the hearing, and asking him to have a look at the file and submit his documents and a note of his defence. The letter has to be accompanied by a copy of the petition and of the explanatory note of it or of the statement of the plaintiff (Article 65 amended by Law No. 18/1989).

125. An original of the petition and copies of it equal to the number of the defendants should be handed over by the clerk to the bailiff. The bailiff has to notify the petition to each defendant.

As a rule, the copy of the petition has to be delivered to the defendant by a bailiff. Egyptian law does not recognize the delivery of the petition by mail, except in rare cases.

The bailiff may hand the copy of the petition to the defendant himself at any place if he knows his identity.

Otherwise, the copy is handed at the defendant's residence. If the defendant is not present at his residence, the copy is handed to any member of his family living in the same residence or to any one of his servants.

In case of refusal to receive the copy, or if the place in which the copy has to be handed over is closed, or if no one who may be handed the copy is present at the residence, the bailiff hands the copy to the mayor or to the police commissioner and sends – within twenty-four hours – a notice by registered mail to the defendant.

126. There are more details in this matter concerning different ways of handling the petition, which vary according to the different situations of the defendant (Article 13 C.Civ.Proc.), as follows:

(1) The copy of the petition against the state, ministers, governors and public juristic persons is to be handed to the 'Department of the State's cases'.
(2) The copy of the petition against a commercial company is to be handed to its legal representation or its general manager.
(3) The copy of the petition against a foreign company, who has a branch or an agent in Egypt, is to be handed to the branch or to the agent.
(4) The copy of a petition against a person serving in the armed forces is to be handed through the general procurator to the 'Judicial Commission of the Armed Forces'.
(5) The copy of a petition against a prisoner is handed to the commander of the prison.
(6) The copy of a petition against a pilot on a commercial ship is handed to the captain.
(7) The copy of the petition against a person having a known residence in a foreign country is handed to the general procurator who sends the papers to the Ministry of Foreign Affairs to hand the copy by diplomatic means through the Egyptian Consul in the foreign country or – if there is reciprocity– through the foreign Consul in Egypt. The bailiff should, within twenty-four hours of handing the copy to the general procurator, send – by registered mail with a notice

of delivery – to the defendant (his address indicated in the petition) a letter informing him that the copy has been delivered to the general procurator. A copy of the petition should be attached to this letter.

(8) If the defendant's domicile or residence is unknown, the plaintiff should indicate the last known address of the defendant, and the copy is handed to the public procurator (Article 13 C.Civ.Proc.).

In all these cases, if the bailiff does not find the person to whom he may hand the copy, or this person refuses to receive it, the bailiff hands the copy to the public procurator.

127. The defendant must be summoned within three months of the registration of the petition; otherwise, the court may consider the petition as non-existent (Article 70 C.Civ.Proc.).

II. Progress of Proceedings

128. Except for Economic Courts, Egyptian law does not know the system of preparation of the trial before a judge or a distinguished member of the chamber. The formal preparation for trial takes place after the notification of the petition to the defendant. According to Article 65/2 (amended by Law No. 18/1999), the defendant, three days before the date of the first session, should deposit in the clerk's office his written defence attached by his documents. In practice, it is rarely submitted then, it is submitted at the first hearing. But even then, if the defendant's lawyer pleads an excuse, he will be given more time. In many hearings, nothing more is accomplished than to fix a date for a subsequent hearing.

During the proceedings before the court, trial preparation is done without formal legal machinery. Defendants or their lawyers have a full opportunity to make a complete presentation of their case on facts and on law, by means of adjournments, which is granted during the ensuing proceedings. The consequence is that frequently issues are not clearly defined until during the trial.

129. By exception, within every preliminary chamber in the Economic Court, a panel is composed to prepare the trial. The panel shall be headed by a judge of the appellate chamber of the Economic Courts and include a sufficient number of judges of the Court of First Instance. The preparation panel shall have the task of verifying completeness of documents related to the disputes, studying these documents, holding hearing sessions for the parties, preparing memoranda of the demands and evidence submitted by the parties, determining the points of agreement or disagreement between them. This task should be executed within thirty days from the date of the registration of the case on the roll. This period may be extended by order of the President of the court. In the process of executing its functions, the preparation panel may resort the assistance of specialized experts (Article 8 Law No. 120/2008).

130. On the other hand, Egypt does not have the jury system, either in criminal or in civil cases. There are some advantages to not having a jury. Trial procedure and rules of evidence are much simpler. There are no problems of jury selection, no challenges to the panel, no difficulties as to the relationship of judge and jury, no motions for directed verdict or judgment notwithstanding the verdict. There is no need to differentiate between 'questions of law' and 'questions of fact', and to give instructions to a body of laymen who are not capable of distinguishing reliable sources of information from unreliable ones (Fathi Waly, *Jury System in the United States of America*, Law and Economy Review, Cairo, 1960).

131. At the hearing, if neither party appears, either personally or by an attorney, the case is held in abeyance, and the case is cancelled until one of the parties goes to the clerk's office in the court and schedules a new hearing to which the defendant is summoned. This must be done within sixty days. If in the new hearing neither party appears, the court announces that the case is deemed non-existent. But this does not forbid the plaintiff re-raising his claim and starts new proceedings. By exception, the court may not hold the case in abeyance if all the parties have submitted their demands, defences and evidence and the court deems that the case is ready to be judged (Article 82/1 C.Civ.Proc. amended by L. 23/92).

132. Sometimes only one of the parties is present, and the other is absent. If it is the plaintiff who is absent, this absence does not present any obstacle for the judge to continue with the case if the defendant so desires (Article 82/2 C.Civ.Proc.).

If the plaintiff is present and the defendant is absent, this does not affect the continuation of the case unless it happens at the first audience. If it is the first audience, the court fixes a date for another hearing and instructs the plaintiff to send a notice to the defendant to be present at this hearing. In the new hearing, the defendant is deemed present even if he does not appear. This rule does not apply if the defendant has received the copy of the petition himself, or if the case is an urgent matter (Article 84 C.Civ.Proc.).

III. Judgment

133. After the demands, defences and all evidence have been received, the court closes the hearings and fixes a date for the rendition of the judgment. The deliberation of the judges begins. They proceed to study the record and discuss their final decision.

After the closure of the hearing, the parties or their lawyers may present no note or document. They have no more contact with the case.

By exception, the court can order the reopening of the debate if there is a serious reason that requires it (Article 173 C.Civ.Proc.). Examples: if reopening of the debate is necessary to enable a party to use his right of defence, or if a judge in the chamber dies during the deliberation.

134. The decision is reached by majority (Article 169 C.Civ.Proc.). The judgment is pronounced publicly through the reading of its terms (Article 174 C.Civ.Proc.). In practice, judgments in civil cases are not pronounced; they are filed in the clerk's office.

135. The judgment has to be written in a certain form. It states the name of the court, the date, the place of the court, whether the case is civil or commercial or relating to urgent matters, the names of judges and of the representative of the public prosecutor if he has attended the hearing, the status, the addresses of parties and their absence or presence. The judgment states briefly the facts, claims, the parties, exceptions, essential defences and demurers. Then, the court gives its legal reasons, upon which the decision is rendered, and the decision proper granting or denying a remedy (Article 178 C.Civ.Proc.).

136. The judgment is anonymous, in the sense that it does not reveal whether it was passed by the majority of the judges or unanimously. The expression of a dissenting opinion is not permitted.

137. On the pronunciation of the judgment, a draft of the judgment has to be deposited in the file of the case. This draft contains the reasons and the decision proper. It should be signed by all the member judges of the chamber, which rendered the decision (Article 175 C.Civ.Proc.). No copies may be taken from this draft (Article 177 C.Civ.Proc.).

An original of the judgment is signed by the judge (or the head of the chamber) and by the clerk (Article 179 C.Civ.Proc.) and is deposited in the file of the case.

After the original of the judgment is filed in the clerk's office, any person may secure an official copy of it after paying the necessary fees (Article 180 C.Civ.Proc.).

138. Once a judgment on the merits is rendered, it is res judicata. This means that the case that has been judged may not be re-judged. The plaintiff may not sue again on the same claim, nor may the defendant enter a plea to bar a case already judged.

According to Article 116 (C.Civ.) the judge has to raise the 'res judicata' 'ex officio'.

The res judicata affects the terms of the judgment. According to the 'Court of Cassation', it also affects the conclusive reasons that are the necessary foundation of the terms. These reasons are called the reasons related closely to the terms.

139. For some authors, the rule of res judicata is based on the presumption of truth attached to the decision of the court (*pro vertitate habietur*).

In fact, this 'res judicata' is a necessary result of the function of the judiciary. The judiciary applies the law in a certain case and offers juridical protection to a certain person against a certain other person concerning a certain object for a claim based on a certain cause. This protection will not be effective in practice if it does not guarantee the stability of the rights and legal positions protected by the judgment. As the law must be respected, even if it is insane or against justice, so must be the judgment which applies the law.

140. A judgment on merits discharges the judge who has pronounced it. But there are three exceptions to this rule:

(1) The court may, by itself (ex officio) or on the demand of the interested party, correct the material mistakes in its judgment, for example, a miscalculation or a mistake on the name of a party. There is no time limit for this correction. The correction is made without hearing and signed by the judge and the clerk. The correction may be challenged by the same means of challenge acceptable against the judgment corrected. If the court refuses the demand for correction, its decision may not be challenged (Article 191 C.Civ.Proc.).
(2) The party may ask the court to interpret the ambiguity of the terms of the judgment. The claim of interpretation is raised as any ordinary claim without a time limit and ends by a new judgment that is considered as complementary of the interpreted judgment. The judgment in the claim of interpretation, whether accepting the claim or not, may be challenged by the same means by which the interpreted judgment may be challenged (Article 192 C.Civ.Proc.).
(3) If the court forgets to render a judgment on one of the claims (*infra petita*), the interested party may return to the court by summoning his adversary to an audience before the court to examine this claim and in adversary proceedings, pronounce judgment on it (Article 193 C.Civ.Proc.).

This return to the same court to decide on a forgotten claim has no time limit. It is accepted as long as the demand forgotten has not been prescribed.

141. This procedure to supplement a judgment is not applied when the court has decided on issues not claimed or has claimed more than was decided (*ultra petita*). In this case, the judgment concerning these issues is void and may be challenged by appeal, exceptionally even if it is originally non-appealable.

IV. Judgment by Default

142. According to the Egyptian Code of 1949, defendants had the possibility to oppose judgments rendered in their absence. The present Code of 1968 has considered the judgment passed in the absence of the defendant as adversarial and, consequently, deprives him of the right to oppose it.

143. To reach this result, the Egyptian Code presented some new rules to assure that the defendant has knowledge of the case. These rules are the following:

(a) If the defendant or his lawyer is present at any audience, the judgment is considered adversarial (Article 83 C.Civ.Proc.).

(b) The judgment is considered adversarial even if the defendant is not present at any audience, if he submits a written note containing his defence, or if he has personally received the copy of the petition (Articles 83–84 C.Civ.Proc.).
(c) If the defendant has been summoned (not in person), and in spite of this the defendant did not appear at the first audience fixed for the hearing of his case, the court has to order a new summons to be served by the 'plaintiff' of the defendant for the new audience (Article 84 C.Civ.Proc.).

By this system, the Code has respected the principle of adversary proceedings without giving any place to judgments by default.

Chapter 3. Challenge of Judgments

144. The general rule is that no action of nullity may be accepted against a judgment. A judgment may be challenged only by means of challenge determined by law, as a part of the judicial structure of the proceedings started by raising the claim.

The Egyptian Code of Civil Procedure recognizes two different kinds of challenges, ordinary challenge and extraordinary challenge. The ordinary challenge is a way to review the case in which the challenged judgment has been rendered. It supposes only that the party has lost his case. The court will have the same power which the court that rendered the judgment had.

On the opposite side, the extraordinary challenge supposes a certain reason for challenge determined by the law. To be accepted, the losing party has to prove one at least of these reasons. The court will not have the same power of the court, which rendered the challenged judgment. It does not review the case, but it investigates whether there is, in the judgment challenged, a reason for challenge determined by law.

Egyptian law knows one way of ordinary challenge, that is the appeal. It knows two ways of extraordinary challenge: cassation and petition for review.

§1. General Principles

145. According to Articles 211–218 (C.Civ.Proc.), there are some general principles which have to be applied at all means of challenge.

These are the following:

(a) Challenge of the judgment is raised only by the party who loses the case totally or partially, and it is not allowed to the losing party who has accepted the judgment, expressly or tacitly (Article 211 C.Civ.Proc.).
(b) Judgments before the end of the process may not be challenged before the pronunciation of the judgment that ends the process. From this rule, the law makes some exceptions, for provisional judgments, decisions of suspension of the instance, judgments which are enforceable instruments, decisions of non-jurisdiction referring the case to the competent court (Article 212 C.Civ.Proc.).
(c) The law fixes a time during which the challenge has to be made. This time limit starts from the date on which the judgment has been rendered unless the law fixes a different starting point. For instance, the time limit starts from the notification of the judgment, if the losing party was absent from all the audiences and has not submitted a note of defence (Article 215 C.Civ.Proc.).
(d) The challenge does not benefit anyone except the challenger. By exception, a challenge of a judgment rendered in an indivisible object, or concerning a co-obligation or rendered in an action in which the law requires the representation of many parties affects others than the challenger (Article 218 C.Civ.Proc.).

§2. APPEAL

146. Appeal aims to have a case judged by a Court of First Instance re-judged by a court of higher rank.

It is the way by which the law applies the principle of the double layer of jurisdiction.

The time limit to appeal is forty days from the date of pronunciation of the judgment. It is fifteen days for judgments in matters of urgency (Article 227 C.Civ.Proc.).

I. Conditions to Appeal

147. The principle is that an appeal is possible against any first instance decision unless it is expressly forbidden by law.

The law does not allow appeal in some cases. These are the cases in the Tribunals of Small Instance the value of which does not exceed EGP 5,000 (Article 42 C.Civ.Proc. amended by Law No. 76/2007) and cases in the Tribunals of Grand Instance the value of which does not exceed EGP 40,000 (Article 47 C.Civ.Proc. amended by Law No. 76/2007).

148. Sometimes, the law prescribes that the judgment is appealable notwithstanding its value: for example, judgments in matters of urgency (Article 220 C.Civ.Proc.), final judgments of first grade which are rendered by a court which has no jurisdiction or which is void for its nullity or for the nullity of the proceedings (Article 221 C.Civ.Proc.), and final judgment rendered in contradiction to a precedent judgment which may be appealed.

II. Appeal Proceedings

149. The proceedings in a Court of Appeal are the same as in the Tribunal of First Grade, with very few variations due to the specificity of the second level of jurisdiction. Therefore, Article 240 (C.Civ.Proc.) prescribes that all procedures and rules of the case in first grade are applied in appeal, except matters for which the law prescribes a different rule.

150. The petition of appeal has to be signed by a lawyer accepted to plead before the Court of Appeal to which the petition is to be submitted.

The petition should contain the same elements as the petition introducing the claim at the first level. However, the petition of appeal must contain, in addition, an indication of the appealed judgment, its date, the reasons of appeal (error both of fact and of law alleged) and summary statement of the claim (Article 230 C.Civ.Proc.).

151. The appeal by which the proceedings at the second level of jurisdiction are initiated is called the main appeal. This main appeal may be supplemented by another appeal from the adversary against the main appeal. This appeal may be a counter-appeal or incidental appeal.

152. The appeal, which is raised by the respondent through the process in the main appeal, is called a counter-appeal. The counter-appeal may be raised during the time limit of the main appeal or after its expiration. On the other hand, it may be raised after the acceptance of the judgment by the respondent or in case of his non-acceptance (Article 237/1 C.Civ.Proc.).

153. The counter-appeal which is raised by the respondent after the time limit of the main appeal, or after his acceptance of the judgment is called an incidental appeal.

This incidental appeal is connected to the main appeal. If the main appeal is void or extinguished for any reason, the incidental appeal is considered non-existent (Article 237/2 C.Civ.Proc.).

The counter-appeal is raised by the respondent against the main appellant. It is not accepted against another respondent.

The counter-appeal is raised by the ordinary proceedings as the main appeal or by a simple note containing its reasons and submitted to the court (Article 237/1 C.Civ.Proc.).

154. New parties, which did not appear in first instance, may not be called into the appeal. The forced intervention of a third party in appeal is strictly forbidden.

A third party may voluntarily intervene, only to join one of the parties in his demand or defence. He may not intervene to submit new demands to the court (Article 236 C.Civ.Proc.).

These rules are based on the desire of the law to respect the principle of the double layer of jurisdiction.

III. Effects of Appeal

155. Appeal has no effect on the enforcement of a judgment. If the judgment has provisional enforcement, it keeps its force even if it has been challenged by appeal (Article 287 C.Civ.Proc.).

156. Appeal transfers the dispute that has already been adjudicated in first instance to the Court of Appeal to be judged again in fact and in law. This effect is called the devolution of the dispute. It applies only to the parts of a judgment, which have been indicated by the appellant (Article 232 C.Civ.Proc.).

If the appellant does not limit the parts of judgment which he wants to appeal, his appeal will apply to all claims judged by the appealed judgment.

157. The appellant may not submit new claims to the Court of Appeal. Any claim that has not been submitted to the Court of First Instance may not be submitted in appeal (Article 235/1 C.Civ.Proc.).

A claim is considered new if it defers, in person or object, of the claims in the first instance.

If it defers only in its reason, it may be, by exception, submitted for the first time in appeal. As an example, if the reason for an action for property is of a contract of sale, its reason may be substituted in appeal by another reason such as succession or a will. An action of liability in tort may be substituted by an action for contractual liability as long as the parties and the object have not been changed.

This rule is called 'no new claims in appeal'. It is based on the desire of the law to respect the principle of a second layer of jurisdiction. If we allow new claims in appeal, this means that the new claim will be judged in only one layer.

158. By exception to this rule, Egyptian law allows certain new demands on appeal, as follows:

(1) The claim of an additional amount of interest or other accessories of the main claim which occurred after the closure of pleadings in first instance.
(2) The claim for liability of the appellant who has raised the appeal, or behaved in appeal out of malice or bad faith.

159. All claims, arguments, defences, exceptions, evidence and documents which have been submitted to the Court of First Instance are deemed submitted to the Court of Appeal.

160. The parties in appeal may submit new arguments, new evidence and new documents to justify in appeal the claims submitted in first instance, or new claims, which they have exceptionally raised to the Court of Appeal.

161. The Court of Appeal has the power to re-judge the case. It has in this aspect the same power, which the Court of First Instance had. The Court of Appeal keeps this power even if the judgment of first instance is null and void. The Court of Appeal, which annuls this judgment, is not discharged of the case on merits. It does not send back the case to the Court of First Instance to judge it.

By exception to this effect, if the act of introducing the proceedings to the Court of First Instance or the notification of this act to the defendant is void, the Court of Appeal has no power to rule on the merits of the case. It should, after declaring the annulment of the judgment, send back the case to the Court of First Instance to judge it.

§3. Petition for Review

162. A petition for review is an extraordinary measure which aims at correcting a judicial mistake based on reasons relating to the facts of the case, and obtaining a new judgment.

Its time limit is forty days starting from the day when the party has had knowledge of the reason for the petition (Article 242 C.Civ.Proc.).

The court which has jurisdiction for review is the same court which rendered the judgment.

I. Reasons of Petition for Review

163. The reasons of petition for revision are fixed strictly by the law as follows: (Article 241 C.Civ.Proc.):

(a) Judgment may be reviewed if it appears after the judgment that it has been rendered due to deception of the party who benefited from it. Deception supposes an act with the intention of deceiving the court.
(b) If the judgment has been based on documents acknowledged as or judicially declared false subsequent to the judgment.
(c) If the judgment has been based on testimony judicially declared false subsequent to the judgment.
(d) If, after the judgment, conclusive documents, which had been kept by the opposite party, have been retrieved.
(e) If the judgment rules on a matter not requested by the parties, or grants the parties more than they have requested.
(f) If the decision proper of the judgment was rendered against a person who has not been properly represented in the case, except in case of contractual representation.
(g) If the judgment affects a natural or juristic person who did not intervene in the case, and his representative has committed fraud, deception or gross negligence.

164. The petition for review may be resorted to only if the judgment is final, either because it is rendered final by a first instance court because the time limit for appeal has elapsed or because it is rendered by a Court of Appeal. If the appeal is possible, it should be used to correct the judicial mistake, and petition for review is not admissible.

A final judgment may be challenged by a petition of review, although it may also be challenged by cassation. The Court of Cassation does not deal with the mistakes of judgment concerning facts.

II. Effects of the Petition

165. A petition for review has no suspense effect. But, the petitioner may ask the court to suspend the enforcement if considerable and unremediable harm would affect the petitioner from the execution of the judgment (Article 245 C.Civ.Proc.).

III. Proceedings for the Petition for Review

166. In the petition for review, the court proceeds through two stages. In the first stage, it examines whether there is a reason for review and whether it has affected the decision. If so, the court accepts the petition. After that, the court starts the second stage. In this case, the court re-examines the case in merit in the light of the correct facts (Article 247 C.Civ.Proc.).

The judgment on the petition for review is subject to the same forms of challenge as the first judgment, except a petition for review. A second petition for review is not accepted (Article 247 C.Civ.Proc.).

§4. Cassation

I. Nature of the Challenge of Cassation

167. The cassation aims to challenge the judgment for non-conformity with the rules of law. Cassation may not challenge the facts of the dispute. The role of the Court of Cassation is to control whether the court ruling on the merits has correctly applied the law applicable to the facts of the dispute.

II. Reasons of Cassation

168. The reasons of cassation are the following (Article 248 C.Civ.Proc.):

(a) Violation of the law or mistake in its application or its interpretation. This reason concerns the qualifications of the facts, the choice of the rule of law applicable to the case, the interpretation of this rule and the adequacy of its application to the facts.

The judge is supposed to know the law. Parties do not have to prove the existence of the rule of law. But this does not extend to foreign laws.

A foreign law, which is applicable to the case, has to be proved by the parties. When the foreign law has been proved, it is considered as a rule of law, and the non-conformity of the judgment to this foreign law is a reason for cassation.

(b) The nullity of the judgment or the nullity of the proceedings which affected the judgment. The lack of reasons, the defect in the reasoning of the judgment or the insufficient reasons concerning the situation, in fact, leads to the nullity of judgment.

(c) The non-jurisdiction of the court which rendered the judgment.

169. The Court of Cassation does not control the finding of the facts or the appreciation of the existence of their elements, which are left to the sovereign appraisal of the court of merits. Therefore, it does not interfere in the interpretation of contracts, the appraisal of the existence of the elements of tort liability.

But the Court of Cassation controls the application of the legal rules of law concerning the interpretation of contracts or concerning the evidence. Therefore, it controls the misinterpretation by the court of merits of clear clauses in a contract or the misapplication of the rules concerning the burden of proof or the power of certain evidence.

In addition, the Court of Cassation controls the logic of the judge of merits in his appraisal of the facts or of the evidence in the case.

III. Judgments Challenged by Cassation

170. The challenge by cassation is possible only against judgments rendered by the courts of appeal. A judgment of the tribunal of first instance is not controlled by cassation even if it is final or even if it became final by the expiration of the time limit of appeal. Such judgment may be challenged by cassation only if it is rendered contrary to a precedent judgment having the force of res judicata and may not be appealed (Article 249 C.Civ.Proc.).

IV. Proceedings in the Court of Cassation

171. The time limit to lodge a challenge in the Court of Cassation is sixty days after the rendering of the judgment, as indicated in the general principles. This time limit does not apply to cassation raised by the public prosecutor (Article 252 C.Civ.Proc.).

172. Neither the time limit nor the raising of the cassation suspends the enforcement of the challenged judgment unless the Court of Cassation orders the suspense of its execution. This order is issued if there would be great and irreparable harm affecting the challenging party due to this enforcement. To be accepted, the request for the suspense should be included in the petition of cassation itself.

If accepted, the enforcement is suspended until the decision in the challenge of cassation is issued. For the cases in which the Court of Cassation suspends the execution, it must fix an audience for the pleadings within six months after the suspension (Article 251 C.Civ.Proc.).

173. The challenge of cassation is raised by a petition submitted to the clerk of the Court of Cassation. The petition has to be signed by an attorney admitted to plead before the Court of Cassation. The parties must also be represented by an attorney in the pleadings at the Court of Cassation. They may not, in all cases, appear in person in the Court of Cassation (Article 266 C.Civ.Proc.). It is not allowed to submit a reason of cassation which has not been included in the petition, by exception of the reasons relating to public interest (Article 253 C.Civ.Proc.).

174. The case is prepared through the exchange of written statements by the lawyers of the parties in the cassation clerk's office. The defendant has to deposit his note of defence within fifteen days of the notification of the petition to him. The challenger may deposit a reply to this defence within fifteen days after the expiration of the above-mentioned time limit. The defendant may deposit his comment within a similar time limit (Article 258 C.Civ.Proc.). No other notes are allowed after these periods (Article 262 C.Civ.Proc.) unless the court – after examining the case – gives permission to the parties to do so (Article 267 C.Civ.Proc.). The public minister then presents his opinion about the reasons of cassation. Article 265 (C.Civ.Proc.) prevents oral observations or defences before the court, but it is the custom that the lawyers give oral speeches to clarify their points of view.

V. Effects of the Challenge of Cassation

175. The cassation, contrary to the appeal, has no devolution effect. New legal arguments, new facts, new evidence, new defence, may not be brought forward in the Court of Cassation. There are some exceptions to this rule:

(a) New legal defence relating to public order is admissible as long as it is drawn from facts or documents which have been presented to the court ruling on the merits.
(b) New defence is accepted if based on defects in the judgment itself.
(c) Defence of public order and purely legal arguments presupposing the facts as established by the court of merits may be raised ex officio by the cassation court.

VI. Effects of the Quashing of a Judgment

176. The quashing of the judgment annihilates it. It places the parties in the situation they were in before the quashed judgment. It also annihilates the judgments and all other acts based on the quashed judgment (Article 271 C.Civ.Proc.). This quashing may be total regarding the judgment in all its parts or partial regarding only a part of it.

If the reason for quashing the judgment is the non-jurisdiction of the court which rendered it, the Court of Cassation fixes the court which has jurisdiction of the case. The interested party may, as he deems fit, raise his action again before this court.

If the reason for quashing the judgment is another different reason, the Court of Cassation sends back the case to the court which has rendered the case to retry it by another chamber. The Court of Cassation, after quashing the judgment, does not retry the case itself (Article 289/142 C.Civ.Proc.).

177. Exceptionally, the Court of Cassation quashes without remitting and retries the case itself in two situations (Article 269 C.Civ.Proc.):

(1) When the cassation is for the second time. This supposes that the Court of Cassation has quashed a judgment and the case has been remitted to the court of merits to be re-judged. If this court issues a new judgment, and this judgment has been challenged for the second time in the Court of Cassation, the Court of Cassation judges itself on the merits to put an end to the dispute.

(2) If the Court of Cassation after quashing the judgment finds that the case can be judged in merits without more pleadings in merits or investigations. In this situation, the Court of Cassation applies the proper rule of law to the facts as they have been appraised by the court of merits without the need for investigation about the facts. There would be no need to send back the case to the court of merits.

178. According to Article 12 Law No. 120/2008 governing the procured before the Economic Cases, as an exception to Article 269 C. Civ. Proc. if the Court of Cassation quashes the judgment, it shall judge the merits of the case, even if the challenge of cassation has been for the first time, or the case needs more investigations or pleadings in merits.

179. The judgment of the Court of Cassation binds the court of merits that will retry the case in the legal issues in which the Court of Cassation states its opinion.

But the court of merits that retries the case regains its full authority concerning the facts.

Decisions of the Court of Cassation do not bind the courts of merits in a case other than the case involved by its decision, but these decisions have the highest respect before these courts.

§5. Opposition by a Third Person

180. According to the Egyptian Code of 1949, the third party had a special means of challenge, the opposition by a third party, which permits him to gain a decision that the judgment would not affect him.

The opposition of a third party was open to anyone who was not a party and was not represented in the proceedings.

181. The present Code of 1968 found that there is no need for this means of challenge because the third party affected by the judgment may always – if he has an interest – raise a case to have a declaratory judgment stating that the judgment does not affect him. Therefore, the present Code disregarded the opposition of a third party as a mean of extraordinary challenge and added some of its reasons as reasons for petition of review (the extraordinary note of the Code of 1968).

This attitude of the present Code is criticized by some Egyptian authors.

Part V. Incidents

182. The suit can be disturbed, suspended, stopped by some events and terminated without passing judgment on the claims raised.

A list of such incidents, without going into details, is the following.

§1. Joinder of Actions

183. The court may order the joinder of several actions brought before it if there is such a link between them that it is in the interest of 'good justice' to examine them together. Such order is an act of judicial administration and may not be appealed.

§2. Discontinuance of the Instance

184. An instance may be discontinued for reasons which relate to the personal aspects of the parties and may affect the principle of adversary pleadings.

The law has determined the causes of the discontinuance as following (Article 130 C.Civ.Proc.):

(1) When one of the natural parties dies, or the juristic person expires.
(2) When the party becomes incapable.
(3) When the party recovers his capacity.

185. According to Egyptian law, the instance does not discontinue when the mandatory representation by the attorney of the party ceases, either by the death of the lawyer or of the termination of his power of attorney.

In this event, the court gives the party sufficient time to prepare his defence, if he has appointed another lawyer within fifteen days of the death or the termination of the power of attorney of the original lawyer (Article 130/3 C.Civ.Proc.).

186. In spite of the existence of a cause for the discontinuance of the instance, this reason does not affect the continuance of the instance, if it happens after the closure of the hearings (Article 131 C.Civ.Proc.).

187. The discontinuance of the instance occurs by the effect of law. It does not require a decision from the court.

When there is discontinuance of instance, the instance resumes when the cause of the discontinuance has disappeared or has been remedied (for details *see* Articles 132 and 133 C.Civ.Proc.).

§3. Suspension of the Instance

188. The instance may be suspended for a certain period. This suspension may be '*legis opis*', judicial or by agreement:

(1) Suspension *legis opis*: this suspension occurs as a result of a certain event. For example, according to Article 162 (C.Civ.Proc.), if there is a request of challenge against the judge, the instance is suspended until the case is decided.
(2) Judicial suspension: this suspension occurs as a result of a judicial decision. The most frequent causes of this suspension are:
   (a) Suspension of the instance as a penalty: the law gives the judge the authority to suspend the instance as a penalty to be imposed on the plaintiff if he does not respect his duties in the instance. This suspension should not exceed one month. If the plaintiff does not comply during that time, his instance is terminated (Article 99 C.Civ.Proc.).
   (b) Suspension until a decision is rendered on a preliminary issue. If an issue has been raised during the instance on the decision of which depends the judgment in the case and this issue is of the jurisdiction of another court, the court has to suspend the instance until a final decision is rendered on this issue by the court having jurisdiction.
(3) Suspension by agreement: the parties may agree to suspend the instance for a certain period not exceeding three months (Article 128 C.Civ.Proc.). This period is sometimes necessary to enable the parties to conclude a conciliation to end the dispute amicably.

§4. Termination of the Instance

189. The instance normally ends as a result of a judgment passed in all the claims.

But, sometimes, the instance ends without a judgment on the claims. This happens for many causes such as conciliation agreed by the parties. Other than conciliation regulated by the Civil Code, the Code of Civil Procedures regulates some causes of termination of the instance. These are as follows.

I. Expiration of the Instance

190. The instance in which the plaintiff has not acted out of negligence for six months expires (Article 134 C.Civ.Proc.). This expiration has to be requested by the defendant. The court may not declare the expiration of the instance ex officio. Once the court declares the expiration of the instance, the instance is deemed expired from the moment the six months has ended.

If the instance is interrupted for reasons related to the plaintiff, the six months starts from the date of the notification by the defendant to the heirs of the plaintiff, to his legal representative or to the plaintiff himself if he has recovered his capacity.

In case of suspension of the instance, the six months starts from the end of the time of suspension if the suspension of the instance is for a limited period, or from the occurrence of the specified event until which the instance has been suspended.

191. The expiration of the instance does not affect the substantial rights of the plaintiff, nor his right of action unless it has been prescribed. The plaintiff may – after the expiration of the instance – start a new one.

The lapse concerns only the procedures. The instance expires with all its acts and the legal effects of these acts.

192. Exceptionally, in spite of the expiration of the instance, some acts of procedure remain.

Those acts are the following:

(a) The judgments on merits rendered during the instance before its expiration.
(b) The statements made and oaths taken during the procedures of the instance by the parties.
(c) Testimonies and reports of experts (Article 137 C.Civ.Proc.).

All the above-mentioned acts may be used by the parties in a new instance in which they raise the same litigation.

II. Time Limitation

193. An instance which does not move for two years lapses (Article 140 C.Civ.Proc.). This sanction applies even if there has been no negligence attributed to the plaintiff. This time limitation may be interrupted or suspended if there is a cause for interruption or suspension of the instance, or if the party proves that he has been prevented through causes beyond his control from acting in the instance. (A judgment of the general gathered civil and commercial chamber of the Court of Cassation 2 March 1988–Case. No. 960/56.)

The time limitation has the same legal effects as the fall of the instance (Cass. 31 January 1980–Cass. No. 1451/48).

III. Withdrawal of the Instance

194. The plaintiff, or the appellant, may withdraw of the instance. This withdrawal has to be accepted by the defendant because the introducing of a claim against him establishes his right to have a judgment refusing this claim.

195. However, the defendant's acceptance of the withdrawal is not necessary in the following cases:

(1) If the defendant has not presented a counter-claim or a defence on merits because this indicates that he has no interest in keeping the instance.
(2) If the defendant has declared his desire expressly or tacitly in the non-continuation of the instance. Therefore, no acceptance is needed if the defendant has requested to withdraw of the instance, or if he has submitted a demurer aiming to end the instance without a decision on the merits, or if he has raised the non-jurisdiction of the court or the nullity of the main claim.
(3) If the defendant has no legitimate interest in refusing the withdrawal. Therefore, there is no need for acceptance of the withdrawal of the appeal if the judgment appealed was rendered totally in his interest, and the time limit of appeal has ended. In this case, the withdrawal will be in his interest because, by this withdrawal, the judgment rendered in his interest will be final.

196. The withdrawal of the instance concerns only the proceedings. The claim may be filed again by new proceedings.

The withdrawal of the instance is different from the renouncement of a certain act of procedure and of the renouncement of the right of action.

Part VI. Legal Costs and Legal Aids

Chapter 1. Legal Costs

197. Litigation requires many expenses. Part of these expenses are the legal costs paid to the court. The party who instigates the proceedings pays a part of these costs in advance.

When the court renders the judgment terminating the proceedings, the judge orders the losing party to pay all the costs of the proceedings, including the attorneys' fees (Article 184/1 C.Civ.Proc.).

If the losing party is more than one, the court may divide the costs between them in equal shares or proportionally to their interest in the case, as it deems convenient (Article 184 C.Civ.Proc.).

198. The court may order the gaining party to pay the costs if his claimed right has been admitted by the losing party, or if the gaining party has caused the spending of useless costs, or if he has left the losing party, ignoring decisive documents which he had in his possession (Article 185 C.Civ.Proc.).

199. If each party has failed in some of his claims, the court may decide that each one of them would pay what he has already spent of costs or to divide the costs between them as it deems suitable. It may also decide that one of them be responsible for all the costs (Article 186 C.Civ.Proc.).

200. In practice, the court never condemns the losing party to pay the real attorneys' fees. The fees ordered are token fees.

Chapter 2. Legal Aid

201. Legal aid is a system by which a party can benefit from the services rendered by the courts without bearing the expenses of a lawsuit. It gives the poor access to justice on an equal footing with the well-off.

Any natural person who has the right of access to justice in Egypt may benefit from this system, whether he is Egyptian or a foreigner.

Legal aid is available in all types of courts and proceedings whether the beneficiary is a plaintiff or a defendant. It offers him the assistance of an attorney without paying his fees, and the non-payment of the expenses of the case.

202. Legal aid is referred to in Article 98 Eg. Con. This article states that 'Law guarantees for poor means for access to justice and to defend their rights'.

This aid has been elaborated by the law in two ways:

(1) by Articles 23–29 of Law No. 90/1944 relating to expenses in civil matters which give a special judicial committee the authority to decide that the party who cannot afford the expenses of the lawsuit should not bear these expenses;
(2) by Articles 93–97 of the Law of Attorneys No. 227/1984, a committee to offer unpaid help to the poor has been established in each filial of the Bar. This help includes raising the law-suites, hearings, investigations of public attorneys, giving legal consultations and drafting contracts. Nominal allowances are paid – for this assistance – by the Bar.

Part VII. Evidence

203. Evidence in Egyptian law is governed by a special law called Law of Evidence No. 25/1968 which regulates both substantial and procedural aspects of evidence.

Chapter 1. Burden of Proof

204. Parties have to bring forward the facts to the court; they also have the burden of proof of these facts because facts may only be taken into account by the court if they have been proved. Without this proof, the judge may not rely on any fact even if he personally knows of its existence and the truth about it.

But the fact brought forward and not challenged by the adversary party does not have to be proved.

The burden of proof lies on the party who brings forward a fact in his interest, whether he is the plaintiff or the defendant.

We have to notice that this rule of the burden of proof is not of public interest, the parties may agree to transfer this burden from one to another even before the litigation.

Chapter 2. The Judge's Authority

205. The authority of the judge concerning the evidence is governed by the following rules:

(a) The judge does not seek the evidence of the fact unproved, but he may order some evidence to complete the evidence submitted by the parties. Thus, the judge, on his own initiative, if he deems the evidence offered by the parties unsatisfactory, may demand witnesses, request from a party a complementary oath, question the party, ask the opinion of an expert, view the premises involved in the litigation.

(b) The judge has complete control of the evidence. The weight of every single evidence is at his discretion, in order that he relies only on his conviction. He may compare the evidence given by both parties and make his own deductions. He has the right to consider whether the evidence is sufficient or not. But this discretional power has two exceptions:
   (1) The judge has no discretion regarding the facts admitted by the controversy party.
   (2) The judge may not abuse his discretional power. His discretion must be based upon reasonable grounds.

(c) The judge may order a certain means of proof, and after that, abolish this order and not execute it (Article 9 L. Evidence 25/1968).

Chapter 3. Admissibility of Evidence

206. In commercial litigations, the proof may be established by any means, even by witnesses.

In civil litigation written – or equivalent – proof of legal acts is required when the obligation stated exceeds EGP 1,000 (Article 60 L. Evidence, amended by Law No. 76/2007).

If the claim contains many obligations, and each one does not exceed this amount, proof may be made by witnesses even if the amount of the gathered obligations exceeds EGP 10,000.

207. Written proof is not necessary when there is prima facie evidence in writing (a commencement of proof). A commencement of proof consists of a document written by the adversary party which indicates the matter at issue and makes the act appear plausible, for example, a letter or an imperfect instrument. This commencement of proof has to be supported by witness evidence (Article 62 L. Evidence) or by mere presumptions.

In cases where a written document is required for proof, it is also possible to prove by a witness if the party has not been able, for material or moral reasons, to obtain written evidence, or if he has lost the document by a reason beyond his control (Article 63 L. Evidence).

208. The law of Evidence admits the proof of facts *stricto sensu* by any means of evidence such as witness evidence, presumptions, or expert reports. It does not require pre-existing written evidence.

Chapter 4. Administration of Evidence

§1. Written Proof

Written papers may be official or private.

209. An official paper is a paper in which an authorized official, or any person authorized to render a public service, states what he has done or what he has received by interested persons, in the limits of his authority and competence (Article 10 L. Evidence).

An official paper is conclusive evidence of what has been stated in it, not only towards the parties of the paper and their heirs but also towards third persons (Article 11 L. Evidence).

An official paper may be challenged only by action of forgery.

210. If a private paper is signed by a person, this person is deemed the author of this paper unless he denies his writing or signature.

The heir of this person is not obliged to deny the signature; he can, under oath, claim ignorance as to the writing or the signature (Article 14 L. Evidence).

The date of the private paper is binding on the signatory and his heirs but not on third persons unless the date is certain. The date of a private paper is certain if it has been stated in another paper with a certain date, or it has been marked by a competent public official.

The private paper has, also, a certain date from the date of death of the latest signatory, or from the date of an event which makes it impossible to be signed before it (Article 15 L. Evidence).

211. A telegram is accepted as evidence if it's original has been signed by the sender. The telegram is supposed to be consistent with the original unless contrary proof is submitted (Article 16 L. Evidence).

212. Merchants' books are considered proof against other merchants, but they are not accepted against non-merchants unless completed by complementary oath (Article 17 L. Evidence).

213. A private paper may be challenged by the party either by arguing that it is not his genuine writing or his signature or by arguing that the paper is forged.

The verification may take place incidentally during the proceedings in the main action, or it may be the main issue in an independent action if there is no rendering lawsuit.

If the court refuses this pretension, it will fine the challenger with a sum of EGP 400–EGP 2,000 (Article 43 L. Evidence, amended by Law No. 18/1999).

A person claiming that an official or private paper is counterfeit may assert his claim either as an incident in the principal action or in an independent action (Articles 49, 59 L. Evidence) if there is no pending lawsuit.

If a claim of forgery is dismissed, the court will fine the claimant from EGP 1,000–EGP 4,000 (Article 56 L. Evidence, amended by Law No. 18/1999).

§2. Production of Written Papers

214. Written papers are usually produced voluntarily by one or the other party. If the party who possesses a paper refuses to produce it, he is forced to do so. A third party to the instance which possesses a paper may also be forced to produce it.

This rule is based upon the principle that everyone must help justice so that the truth be known. Anyone who, without a legitimate reason, does not comply with this obligation when he is required to do so may be forced to comply with it.

215. According to Article 20 (L. Evidence), the party may ask the court to order the other party to produce a paper possessed by him if it is effective to prove the facts disputed, in the following cases:

(a) If any text of law obliges him to produce the paper, for example, Article 28 of Commercial Code (Law No. 17/1999) prescribes that the judge may order the merchant to produce his books to the court to be used as proof.
(b) If the documents are in common between the party and his adversary.
(c) If the documents have been relied on by his adversary at any stage of the litigation.

216. If the party refuses to produce the document in spite of the order, he must swear that the paper alleged does not exist, that he has no knowledge of its existence or where it exists, that he has not hidden it and did not neglect to search for it with the intention of preventing the adversary party from obtaining it. If the party also refuses to take the oath, the copy of the paper presented to the court is deemed as the original. If the party has not presented a copy, the judge may accept his declaration as to the form and contents of the paper (Articles 23–24 L. Evidence).

217. According to Article 26 (L. Evidence) if the paper is in possession of a third person, the judge may authorize the interested party to intervene in the proceedings, under the penalty of a fine, in the cases mentioned above.

Actio ad exhibendum

218. Besides those articles concerning forced production of papers, Article 27 (L. Evidence) adopts what is known as *actio ad exhibendum.* According to this article, any person who is in possession of documents or other papers relating to a pretended right may be obliged by an injunction of the judge to produce them in the interest of any party who has an interest in relying upon them for the proof of his right.

The possession of the paper may always challenge the judge's injunction for a legitimate reason such as professional or familial secrecy.

§3. Witness Evidence

219. A witness is a person, other than the parties, called to the court to state orally what he knows about the facts of the litigation.

A party is prohibited from testifying. He may not take the witness stand on his own behalf. The reason for this prohibition is to avoid a conflict of interests. The same prohibition is applied to the lawyer or the legal representative of the party. But husband or wife of either party, descendants, ancestors and relatives of either party may testify.

220. The witness should have the capacity to testify. A minor, aged under fifteen years, is not accepted to testify, but the judge may hear his testimony without an oath. This testimony is treated not as proof but as a source of information.

Persons who, as a result of mental capacity or being too young or too old, do not understand what they testify are not capable of testifying.

Also, those who are deprived of their civil rights by a criminal sentence may not testify.

221. Some persons, although capable of testifying, are forbidden from being witnesses of some facts, as follows:

(a) Officials or persons charged with public service may not testify about facts they have known during and as a result of their functions, without the permission of a competent public authority (Article 65 L. Evidence).
(b) Professional persons who obtained confidential information in the course of a professional relationship unless this information is provided in order to commit a crime, or unless the person who gave such information gave permission to reveal it (Article 66 L. Evidence).
(c) The husband or wife regarding the information obtained from each other during the marriage, except in claims raised by one of them against the other or in crimes committed by one against the other (Article 67 L. Evidence).

Inquiry

222. The witness is usually heard in the course of the instance by a procedure called an inquiry.

The inquiry is ordered by the court at the request of the party or ex officio (Article 70 L. Evidence).

The order which permits a party to prove a fact by testimony permits *ipso facto* the adversary to deny it by testimony (Article 69 L. Evidence).

The judgment which orders an inquiry must state the facts to be proved, the date on which the inquiry starts and its time limit (Article 70 L. Evidence).

If the court is composed of more than one judge, one of the judges may be charged to hear the witnesses (Article 72 L. Evidence).

223. The evidence of the witnesses is given in an adversary manner. The witness is summoned before the court or the judge for the designated day. If he does not appear on the designated day, he is sentenced to a fine not exceeding EGP 200. If he appears and refuses to take the oath or to testify, he is sentenced to a fine of EGP 200 (Articles 78, 80 L. Evidence).

When a witness is unable to appear, the judge may conduct the hearing wherever the witness is (Article 81 L. Evidence).

224. The witness gives his testimony orally; he may not use written notes, except with the permission of the judge (Article 90 L. Evidence). This usually occurs when the nature of the action requires the witness to state dates, figures or other details which he is unable to remember without the use of written notes.

In order to prevent collusion, witnesses are interrogated one at a time, the witness testifies without the presence of other witnesses (Article 84 L. Evidence). The witness is excluded from the courtroom until he is called to testify.

If the witness does not understand Arabic, he shall be questioned through an interpreter. If the witness is deaf, dumb, or both, the questions, answers, or both, shall be in writing.

225. The powers of the judge in the inquiry are large. He interrogates the witnesses. He may confront witnesses with one another.

Questions are asked by the judge. The witness should answer first the questions of the party who summons him for testimony, and then the questions of the other party (Article 87 L. Evidence).

The court clerk draws up a record of all the stages of the inquiry and of the evidence from the judge's dictation.

The testimony of the witness should be read to him and signed by him. If he refuses to sign, the reason for this refusal should be indicated in the record (Article 91 L. Evidence).

226. According to Article 96 (L. Evidence), any person may request the testimony of a witness about facts for use in a case which may be brought in the future.

The jurisdiction for this request is for the court of urgent matters. After hearing the witness, the court shall prepare a record stating the evidence of the witness. When the litigation in merits is started, the interested party may obtain a copy of this record and submit it to the court. All objections to the admissibility of proof by testimony shall be raised in front of this court. The adversary party will have the right to bring denying witnesses (Articles 96, 97 L. Evidence).

§4. Questioning of the Parties

227. The court may question any party either on request of the other party or ex officio (Articles 105, 106 L. Evidence). If the party is incompetent, the court may question his representative. If the case involves a juristic person, the questioning shall be addressed to his legal representative.

In any case, the person questioned should be capable of disposing of the right in litigation (Article 107 L. Evidence).

228. The person to be questioned must appear in person at the hearing for the questioning.

Questions are asked by the judge. If the other party has questions to be asked, these questions are proposed to the judge who directs them to the person being questioned. Answers to the questions should be answered in the same audience unless the judge agrees to postpone them (Article 109 L. Evidence).

In all cases, answers should be declared in the presence of the other party who has requested the questioning. But if he failed to appear, questioning will go ahead (Article 110 L. Evidence).

229. The questioning is recorded by the clerk in detail in the audience's record. After being read in the presence of the parties, it shall be signed by the judge, the clerk and the party who was questioned. If the party refuses to sign, a record of this fact shall be made (Article 111 L. Evidence).

230. The questioning is not a direct means of evidence; it is designed to throw light on the facts of the dispute.

But, if the party to be questioned fails to appear without good reason, or refuses to answer the question without legal justification, the court may accept the proof by testimony or by presumptions in cases where the proof should be written (Article 113 L. Evidence).

§5. Proof by Oath

231. Egyptian law regulates two kinds of oaths of the party as proof, decisive oath tendered by the party and completive oath tendered by the court itself.

I. Decisive Oath

232. A decisive oath is tendered by a party to his opponent party to make decisive proof of an essential fact. Each party has the right to tender a decisive oath to the other party, but the judge may not allow the party to tender the oath if he abuses this right (Article 114/1 L. Evidence).

A decisive oath may not be tendered about a fact violating the public order. It may only be tendered to the other party on a personal fact. If it is not personal, the oath will be directed only to his knowledge of the fact and not to its validity. The party who tenders the oath should have the capacity to dispose of the right concerned (Article 115 L. Evidence).

233. The party who wants to tender a decisive oath to his opponent must present the facts about which he renders the oath and determines the phrase of the oath clearly (Article 122 L. Evidence). The court may amend the phrase proposed by the party to make it more clear (Article 123 L. Evidence).

234. The party to whom an oath tendered must either accept to swear or refer the oath to his opponent. A party who refuses an oath tendered to him or refuses to refer it to his opponent loses the point which is the object of the oath. He is also deemed the loser if he did not appear to swear without an acceptable excuse. Similarly, the opponent to whom an oath has been referred who refuses to swear shall lose the point in issue (Article 124 L. Evidence).

A party may not refer the oath to his opponent unless the fact which is the object of the oath is common between the two parties (Article 114/2 L. Evidence).

235. The procedure of tendering a decisive oath to the opponent is too dangerous to use if ordinary evidence is available. It puts the power to decide the case in the hands of the opponent. The temptation to exercise it corruptly is one which only a very conscientious or religious man could resist. Therefore, the party should not tender a decisive oath to his opponent unless in exceptional situations where other evidence of the crucial facts are completely lacking.

II. Completive Oath

236. The completive oath is administrated by the court, on the request of any party or ex officio when the fact to be investigated is not proved by conclusive evidence and the proof offered is not convincing to the judge.

237. The party to whom is tendered a completive oath may accept or refuse to swear, but he may not refer it to his opponent (Article 120 L. Evidence).

The completive oath may concern the value of an object in litigation.

In this case, the judge must fix the maximum value. An oath concerning the value may be tendered only if it is impossible to estimate the value by other means (Article 121 L. Evidence).

When a completive oath is tendered by the court, the court may not render its decision on the merits or on the value before the oath has been accepted or refused.

§6. View of Premises

238. Sometimes it is necessary for the judge to view the premises involved in litigation. By this means, he can verify for himself the facts in dispute. Viewing premises may be ordered either upon the request of a party or upon the court's own initiative (Article 131 L. Evidence).

Although this means is a very efficient way to know the truth, judges are reluctant to make use of it, as it is time-consuming.

239. The viewing of premises is performed either by the court or by one of its delegated members.

The judge fixes the time when he will view the premises; the clerk gives the parties or their lawyers a notice to attend. At the time fixed, the judge goes to the premises with the court's clerk. He may assign an expert to assist him, hear witnesses on the spot (Article 132 L. Evidence). All procedures concerning the viewing of premises must be recorded (Article 131/2 L. Evidence).

§7. Expert Evidence

240. When the judge needs information on facts requiring special technical knowledge, he may ask the opinion of an expert.

Expert opinion may only be requested concerning facts. An expert may not give his opinion – except for foreign law – on legal issues because the judge is supposed to know the law. In practice, judges are tempted to use expert evidence not only for technical facts but also to carry investigations concerning legal issues.

241. The judge may ask the opinion of experts, either on the request of one of the parties or ex officio.

The parties have no power to subpoena any expert, but only the right to suggest to the judge that expert evidence is needed.

The judge has wide discretion; there are no rigid rules as to what matters are properly within the scope of expert evidence. The expert opinion is freely sought. But according to decisions from the Egyptian Court of Cassation, if the matter is a technical one which only specialized people know, and the judge relies on this matter in his judgment, without asking the opinion of an expert, his judgment is void because the judge cannot have knowledge of this matter without the opinion of an expert (Civ.Cass. 26 March 1964-Civ.Cass. Rep. 15-395-66).

242. If the parties are not in accord, the expert is chosen by the court. The court chooses one or three experts from the list of governmental experts accepted before it unless there are special circumstances which require experts, not on this list (Article 136). If the expert chosen is not on the list of experts he has to swear an oath in front of the judge of temporary matters to the effect that this work will be truthful and honest (Article 139 L. Evidence).

When the judge orders an expert appraisal, he decides which party will have to bear the costs. He fixes an amount of money to be paid in advance, but this amount may later be increased.

243. Expert proceedings are regulated in detail by the Egyptian Evidence Law (Articles 135–162).

When the judge appoints the expert, he fixes two dates for two hearings, the first if the party who is committed to paying the expenses of the expert did not pay it, and the second – if the party paid – for the expert's report to be submitted to the court. The date for submission of the report often turns out to be optimistic, with the consequent necessity of postponed hearings.

244. The nominated expert designed may – within five days of his assignment – ask the judge to excuse him on acceptable personal grounds (Article 140 L. Evidence).

Experts may be challenged for almost the same reasons as judges. The challenge must be made within three days of the nomination of the experts if the party is present, or of the notification of this nomination if he is not present (Article 142 L. Evidence). The challenge is decided by the judge who has nominated the expert as an incident. His decision on it may not be appealed. If the judge refuses the challenge of the expert, the party who has raised it is exposed to a fine of EGP 100–EGP 400 (Article 145 L. Evidence).

245. Expert proceedings are adversary. The expert has to notify the parties, by a registered letter, of the place and the hour of the first meeting, at least seven days before the meeting. If the principle of adversary proceedings are not respected, the report of the expert is void (Article 146 L. Evidence).

The expert questions the parties, listens to their observations, makes such tests and experiments as he wishes, and visits such places as are necessary. He may also hear witnesses, without an oath.

246. When the expert ends his work, he writes a report which he submits to the court. The expert's report shall contain the presence of the parties, their observations and those of others heard by the expert, all that the expert has done to perform his work, and the expert's opinion on matters referred to him. The expert's opinion must be reasoned to enable the judge and the parties to consider it. The report should be dated and signed by the expert or experts (Articles 150–151 L. Evidence).

The expert's report has to be handed in the clerk's office. The parties are notified of the deposit of the record, by registered letter (Article 151 L. Evidence).

247. Usually, experts do not appear in court except rarely if the judge asks them to appear to answer questions about their written reports. According to Article 155 (L. Evidence), the court may appoint an expert to submit an oral opinion at the hearing, without writing a report. In this case, his opinion is stated in the record of the hearing.

248. If the expert's written report is inadequate or unsatisfactory, the judge may, ex officio or at the request of one of the parties, decide to return the report to the expert or to appoint another expert or three other experts.

If so, the same procedure is followed as with the first report. If a new expert – or experts – is appointed, a contradictory report may be rendered. When this happens, the judge may accept either one of the reports if convinced of its reliability. He may also appoint a third expert or three other experts.

249. The judge is not bound by the expert's opinion (Article 156 L. Evidence). He has wide discretion in this regard.

Part VIII. Particular Proceedings

250. The proceedings described above are the ordinary proceedings, but Egyptian law organizes particular proceedings to be followed in special matters. The most frequent of those particular proceedings are the following.

Chapter 1. Non-contentious Matters

251. The Egyptian Code of Civil and Commercial Procedures organizes the proceedings in non-contentious matters in Articles 194–200, under the title 'Orders upon requests'.

The law sometimes demands in the absence of dispute because of the nature of the matter or of the quality of the petitioner, that the matter should be submitted to the judge's control, confirmation or authorization. For instance, a declaration of the death of a person, an authorization for the selling of real estate belonging to a minor, a ratification of a settlement, an authorization of seizure of movable properties.

According to a new rule in this Code, the judge may not issue the order except in certain cases determined by law (Article 194 C.Civ.Proc. amended by Law No. 23/1992).

252. The essential characteristic of non-continuous matters is that there is no dispute between two opposing parties. Therefore, there is no place to apply the principle of adversary. This characteristic determines the non-contentious proceedings.

There is only a petitioner who submits a request to the judge. No defendant is summoned, and no hearing takes place before a judge.

According to Article 194 (C.Civ.Proc.), the request is presented either to the judge of provisional matters in the competent court, or to the chief of the chamber dealing with the claim on merits. If the order upon request concerns matters subject to the jurisdiction of an Economic Court, the request should be presented to a judge of this court delegated to this function by the general assembly of the Economic Court at the beginning of each year (Article 3 Law No. 120/2008). The request is presented in duplicate containing the facts of the request, the reasons and the elected domicile of the petitioner in the city where the court is situated. It must be accompanied by instruments of proof.

The law does not require that the request be presented or signed by an attorney.

253. The judge has extensive power to refuse the request. He grants the requested order if he finds that it is needed for the protection of the interest to be protected.

The judge must decide upon the facts and documents presented to him after verifying them. He may not look for facts or for evidence not brought to him by the petitioner. No intervention of a third party is allowed. The public minister is not informed of the request and has no opportunity to present his opinion.

254. The judge must issue a written decision, granting or refusing the order, on one of the two copies of the request, no later than the second day of its presentation to the clerk.

He is not obliged to state reasons for his decision unless it is contrary to a precedent one (Article 195 C.Civ.Proc.).

The clerk must hand the petitioner the second copy of the request carrying the copy of the judge's decision, no later than the second day of rendering the decision (Article 196 C.Civ.Proc.).

255. The interested person – even if he is a third party – may raise an objection against the decision before the court which has jurisdiction of the merits, or before the judge who has issued the decision, within ten days of the decision refusing the order or of the notification or execution of the order, according to the cases (Articles 197 and 199 C.Civ.Proc.).

The order has to be presented for execution within thirty days of issue; otherwise, it falls. This fall does not forbid the right to re-request an order in the same matter and the same demand (Article 200 C.Civ.Proc.).

Chapter 2. Orders of Payment

256. If the right of the plaintiff is stated in a written document signed by the debtor, due promptly, and having as object a determined sum of money or a movable asset determined by itself, by its kind or by its amount, the plaintiff may not follow the ordinary proceedings. He should submit his claim by the following proceedings (Article 201 C.Civ.Proc.).

257. First, he must send a notice to his debtor to pay the debt. This notice is sent by a registered letter with proof of delivery.

After this notice, the creditor starts summary proceedings to obtain an order of payment before the judge of small instances or before the chief of the chamber at the Tribunal of Grand Instances according to the value of the claim (Article 202 C.Civ.Proc.). In Economic Courts, the issuing of the order of payments is in the competence of a judge of this court delegated to this function by the general assembly of the Economic Court at the beginning of each year, regardless of the value of the claim (Article 3 Law No. 120/2008).

The claim is presented in the form of a request in duplicate containing the facts of the claim, the reason, the complete name of the debtor and his domicile, and an elected domicile of the creditor in the city where the court is situated if his residence is outside the jurisdiction of the court. It must be accompanied by documents proving the claim. The request is not notified to the defendant.

258. The judge examines the claim in a non-controversy procedure. He relies upon the facts brought to him in the request and the documents attached to it.

If the judge is convinced of the existence of the creditor's right, he issues an order of payment. This order is issued on a copy of the request within three days from its presentation to the clerk. The order has to determine the original debt and its interest ordered to be paid, or the assets ordered to be delivered, and the expenses of the proceedings (Article 203 C.Civ.).

259. If the judge decides not to accept the claim entirely, he does not issue any decision of refusal or of non-admissibility. He must abstain from issuing any order, and fixes a date for the hearing of the claim before the tribunal which has jurisdiction. The claimant must then notify the date of the hearing to the defendant. The case will be examined in adversary according to the ordinary proceedings (Article 204 C.Civ.Proc.).

If the judge issues an order of payment, the order must be notified to the debtor in person or at his domicile, along with the request upon which it has been put, within three months of being issued. Otherwise, the order becomes invalid and has no effect (Article 205 C.Civ.Proc.).

260. The debtor against whom the order has been issued may raise an objection against the order within ten days from this notification. The objection is raised according to ordinary proceedings, to the tribunal which has jurisdiction either of small or of grand instances. If the debtor who objected fails to attend the first audience, the court declares – ex officio – the objection as non-existent (Article 207 C.Civ.Proc.).

The debtor may also challenge the order of payment by an appeal – if it is appealable – before the appellate court. The time limit of appeal is forty days. It starts from the expiration of the time limit of objection or of the lapse of the objection. If the debtor raises an appeal against the order, his right of objection expires (Article 206 C.Civ.Proc.).

Part IX. Enforcement of Judgments and Preliminary Seizure for Security

261. The Egyptian Code of Civil and Commercial Procedure has provided its second book for the enforcement of judgments and preliminary seizure for security (Articles 274–486).

Chapter 1. General Rules

§1. The Judge of Execution and the Execution Officer

I. The Execution's Administration

262. According to Egyptian law, enforcement of a judgment proceeds under the supervision of an Administration of execution established in each Tribunal of Grand Instance (Mahkama Kulia). It may have, by a decree of Minister of Justice, branches in Tribunals of Small instance (Mahkama Guzeia).

The Administration of execution is headed by an Appellee judge aided by judges delegated by the General Assembly of the Court called judges of execution (Article 274 C.Civ.Proc. amended by Law No. 76/2007).

The Administration supervise the execution. Either the head of administration or the judges of execution has the exclusive competence to issue orders concerning the execution. These orders may be challenged before the head of the Administration whose decision shall be final (Article 274 C.Civ.Proc. amended by Law No. 76/2007).

II. The Judge of Execution

263. According to Article 275 C.Civ.Proc., the judge of execution has exclusive jurisdiction for all contests of forced execution whether the contest is temporary or on merits (Article 275 C.Civ. Proc. Amended by Law No. 76/2007). If the contest concerns decisions issued by Economic Courts, the preliminary chambers in this courts will have exclusive jurisdiction of the contests whether temporary or on merits (Article 7 Law No. 120/2008).

The territorial jurisdiction for the seizure of personal or real property is where the enforcement takes place.

For the seizure of property possessed by a third party or of an intangible property, the territorial jurisdiction is where the third party has his domicile (Article 276 C.Civ.Proc.).

264. The decision of the judge of execution concerning contests on merits, regardless of its value, may be appealed to the Tribunal of Grand Instance (Mahakama Ibitidaia).

The decision concerning a temporary contest may be appealed; it is also appealed to the Tribunal of Grand Instance (Article 277 C.Civ.Proc. amended by Law No. 76/2007).

III. The Execution Officer

265. The execution is proceeded by an execution officer according to Egyptian law. The officer is obliged to execute the judgment at the request of the creditor when he hands him the enforceable instrument.

The execution officer works under the supervision of the Administration of execution.

If the execution officer refuses to accomplish any act of execution, the creditor may complain to the head of administration of execution.

The execution officer may ask the assistance of the police and the local authority, and he may take all the security measures which he deems necessary (Article 279 C.Civ.Proc. amended by Law No. 76/2007).

§2. The Enforceable Instruments

266. The creditor may not enforce the execution of his right unless he has an enforceable instrument stating a certain prompt right and having a determined object (Article 280/1 C.Civ.Proc.).

According to Article 280/2 (C.Civ.Proc.), the enforceable instruments are determined by law. The legislator may give the force of enforceable instrument to any act. The most common enforceable instruments are: judgments, judicial orders, arbitration awards with exequatur, deeds drawn up by a notary.

267. The enforceable instrument must be stamped by an executory formula stating that the authority charged with the obligation of the execution of the enforceable instrument must proceed for execution if it has been asked for, and all competent authorities must help him to do so even by using force when required to do so (Article 280/3 C.Civ.Proc.).

268. The enforceable instrument has to be notified to the debtor in person or at his domicile before the beginning of the enforcement proceedings. The writ of notification must include a summons to the debtor to pay the debt.

The proceedings of execution may start only after at least one day from the notification of the enforceable instrument to the debtor (Article 281 C.Civ.Proc.).

§3. The Judicial Judgment as an Enforceable Instrument

269. The judicial judgment is not considered as an enforceable instrument unless it is final or is granted the power of provisional enforcement (Article 287 C.Civ.Proc.).

270. According to Egyptian law, the provisional enforcement is granted to the judgment either by law or by order of the judge.

The provisional enforcement is granted by law to judgments rendered in some specified matters, the most important of which are urgent matters (Article 288 C.Civ.Proc.) and commercial disputes (Article 289 C.Civ.Proc.).

It is granted by order of the judge in certain cases determined in Article 290 (C.Civ.Proc.), and generally, if the delay of execution would cause great prejudice to the interest of the gaining party (Article 290/6 C.Civ.Proc.).

271. The challenge of the judgment does not automatically stay the execution of the judgment. But a stay of the challenged judgment may be granted by the appellate court for the judgments which have provisional enforcement or by the Court of Cassation for final judgments, rendered by the Court of Appeal upon a party's request (Article 251 and Article 291 C.Civ.Proc.).

§4. Object of Seizure

272. The creditor may seize any property of his debtor, or of a third party if the property is a guarantee for the debt.

For social purposes, the law does not allow the seizure of some properties. The seizure of these properties is void.

The properties which are exempt of seizure are mainly: the necessary clothing and beds for the debtor and his family living with him, the tools and books necessary for the debtor's personal work or profession, female animals necessary for the use of the debtor and his family, a portion of salaries and wages (Articles 305, etc., C.Civ.Proc.). According to Article 4 of the new Investment Law No. 72/2017, the properties of the investment projects may not be seized except by a final judgement or a judicial order, with the exception of taxes and social insurance debts due to the government. This rule also applies to temporary execution. A non-final judgement, even in urgent matters, is not sufficient.

273. The creditor may seize the seizable properties, as he desires, regardless of the amount of his credit.

If he seizes more than he needs to recover his debts, the debtor may ask the judge of execution to limit the seizure to a portion of the seized properties sufficient to cover the debt (Article 304 C.Civ.Proc.). The debtor may also – in that case – deposit a sum of money equivalent to the original debt, interest and expenses of the seizure, with the tribunal, to which the seize is transferred, and the properties seized are liberated of the seizure (Article 302 C.Civ.Proc.). If there is a dispute about the amount of the debt, the debtor may ask the judge of execution to fix the amount of money to be deposited to liberate the properties seized (Article 304).

In all these cases, the creditor will have priority to recover his credit from the properties to which the seizure has been limited or from the money deposited (Articles 302–304 C.Civ.Proc.).

§5. Preliminary Seizure for Security

274. To have the right to a provisional seizure, the creditor has to fulfil the following conditions (Articles 319–325–326 C.Civ.Proc.):

(1) The debt has to be certain and prompt. The certainty of the debt is at the discretion of the judge of execution when he is asked to render an order of provisional seizure. He looks at what appears from the documents presented to him, which shows that the debt is apparently well-founded.

(2) The amount of debt has to be determined. If it is not, the creditor must obtain an order from the judge of execution to determine the amount for which the seizure may be proceeded.
(3) The creditor must have a non-enforceable instrument or a non-enforceable judgment or should obtain an order from the judge of execution, permitting the provisional seizure.

This order is rendered upon a request presented by the creditor according to the proceedings of orders upon requests.

If these three conditions have been fulfilled, the creditor may proceed with the seizure of the rights of his debtors or of his movable properties possessed by a third person without any additional condition.

But if he wants to proceed with the seizure of his debtor's movable properties now possessed by a third party, without having an enforceable instrument or a non-enforceable judgment he should show to whom he asks for permission for a preliminary seizure for security, that certain circumstances could cause the loss of the guarantees of his right (Article 316 C.Civ.Proc.).

This last condition is not applied to the bearer of a bill of exchange or a promissory note if the debtor who signed the bill or the promissory note is a merchant. On the other hand, this condition does not apply if the creditor is the lessor of real estate and wants to seize the furniture or the crops and fruits existing at the real estate leased.

§6. Judgment of Validity and Efficacy of Provisional Seizure

275. If the creditor has executed the provisional seizure without having an enforceable instrument or a non-enforceable judgment, he shall raise – within eight days of the seizure – an action with the judge of execution called 'action of validity and efficacy of provisional seizure'. By this action, the creditor asks the judge for a judgment which declares the debt well-founded and the validity of the proceedings of the seizure.

If this action has not been raised within the time limit, the seizure lapses (Articles 320/3–333 C.Civ.Proc.).

Chapter 2. Proceedings

§1. Kinds of Seizure

276. There are three types of seizure in Egyptian law:

(1) Seizure of rights of the debtor or of his movable properties possessed by a third person.
(2) Seizure of movable properties possessed by the debtor.
(3) Seizure of immovable properties.

The seizure of rights of the debtors or of his properties possessed by a third person, as well as the seizure of movable property not possessed by a third party, may be proceeded by the creditor even if he does not have an enforceable instrument. Each of them may be proceeded either as a means of enforcement or as a protective measure (provisional seizure).

On the contrary, the seizure of immovable properties may not be proceeded unless the creditor has an enforceable instrument. It is always a means of enforcement.

§2. Seizure of Rights or of Movable Material Properties Possessed by a Third Person

277. The seizure of rights or of movable material properties possessed by a third person always starts as a preliminary seizure for security. It starts without a pre-notification of an enforceable instrument to the debtor and without a pre-summons to him in order to pay the debt.

The seizure is executed by a mere notification to the third party by a bailiff of a paper called a 'paper of seizure'.

This paper must contain (Article 328 C.Civ.Proc.):

(1) A copy of the enforceable instrument or the non-enforceable judgment or of the order of the judge permitting the seizure and of his order determining the amount of money for which the seizure may be proceeded.
(2) The amount of money for which the seizure is proceeding.
(3) A summons to the third person not to pay what the debtor owes him, or to hand the debtor his property which the third party possesses.
(4) The determination of the properties or the debts seized.
(5) A choice of an elected domicile in the city where the court of the third person's residence is situated.
(6) A request to the third party to state within fifteen days what the debtor owes him or the debtor's properties which he possesses.

278. Within eight days of this notification, by which the seizure has been executed, the creditor should inform the debtor of it. This information has to be given by a bailiff. If the debtor has not been informed of the seizure within the time limit, the seizure lapses (Article 332 C.Civ.Proc.).

279. If the third party did not state within the time limit what he has for the debtor, or if he hides the truth, or if he did not attach the necessary documents relating to his statement, the judge of execution – at the request of the creditor – may condemn the third party to pay to the creditor the amount of money for which the seizure has been executed (Article 343 C.Civ.Proc.).

280. When the third person presents a positive statement, indicating the amount of money which the debtor owes him, he should – within fifteen days – pay the creditor his debt out of that amount as long as the creditor has obtained an enforceable instrument (Article 344 C.Civ.Proc.). If the third person does not do so, the creditor shall have the right to seize his own properties (Article 346 C.Civ.Proc.).

When the seizure concerns movable properties which the third party possesses according to his statement, these properties will be sold by public auction under the supervision of an execution officer (Article 347 C.Civ.Proc.).

§3. Seizure of Movable Material Properties Possessed by the Debtor

281. The movable material properties possessed by a third person are seized by a paper written by the execution officer in the place where the movable properties exist. In this paper, the execution officer draws up an inventory of the debtors' movable properties in details. He also indicates the enforceable instrument, an elected domicile of the creditor in the city where and the Tribunal of Small Instance is situated in which district the property is located, the place of the seizure and the procedures he has accomplished, and he indicates the day, hour and place of sale. The paper of seizure must be signed by the execution officer and by the debtor if he is present (Article 353 C.Civ.Proc.).

A copy of that paper is handed to the debtor or notified to him not later than the next day of the seizure (Article 362 C.Civ.Proc.).

If the execution officer faces a dispute which he deems serious, he shall refer to the execution's administration. In this case, the execution officer may stay the seizure temporarily.

282. The properties seized are sold by the execution officer in a public auction.

The sale may not be performed before eight days from the handing or the notification of the paper of the seizure to the debtor (Article 376 C.Civ.Proc.).

The execution officer should stay the sale if the price of the properties already sold is sufficient to cover the debt for which the seizure has been executed and the expenses of the proceedings (Article 390 C.Civ.Proc.).

§4. Seizure of Shares, Bonds and Revenues

283. According to Egyptian law, these properties are seized either by the procedures of the seizure of properties possessed by a third person or by the procedures of the seizure of properties possessed by the debtor (Articles 398–399 C.Civ.Proc.).

284. The shares and the bonds for the bearer or endorsable bonds are seized by the procedures of seizure of properties possessed by the debtor if their instruments are not in possession of a third person.

The permanent or provisional revenues, the nominal shares, the shares in profits of juristic persons, the rights of partnerships are seized by the procedures of seizure of properties possessed by a third person.

285. The sale of these properties may be made by a bank or a broker, designated by order of the judge of execution, at the request of the creditor (Article 400 C.Civ.Proc.).

§5. Seizure of Real Property

286. The proceedings of seizure of real property start by an order to pay served by the bailiff to the debtor in person or at his domicile, containing an indication of the enforceable instrument, its date, the amount of the debt to be paid, the date of the notification of the enforceable instrument, a summons to the debtor to pay the debt; otherwise, the order will be registered, and his real property will be sold. The order should contain the particulars of the property seized in detail and a selected domicile for the creditor who is in charge of the proceedings in the town in which the court of execution is located (Article 401 C.Civ.Proc.).

This order should be registered in the real estate registry's office of the place where the property is located (Article 402 C.Civ.Proc.). By this registration, the property is deemed seized (Article 404 C.Civ.Proc.) and, as an effect, any legal disposition of the property will have no legal effect on the seizing creditors, the creditors whose real guarantees have been registered before the registration of the order, and on the person acquiring the property seized, when sold at an auction.

287. Within ninety days of the registration of the order to pay, the creditor in charge of proceedings should hand to the clerk of the court of execution a list containing the particulars of the sale; otherwise, the registration expires. This list should contain the indication of the enforceable instrument, the date of the order, the reserve price, the property indicated in the order in detail, the conditions of the auction (Article 414 C.Civ.Proc.). It should be attached to the documents proving the validity of these elements.

The reserve price is fixed according to the rules of evaluation adopted by Article 37 (C.Civ.Proc.) for the evaluation of the claims for purpose to determine the subject matter jurisdiction of the courts (Article 415 C.Civ.Proc.).

288. A summons should then be served, within fifteen days of the deposit of the list, by a bailiff to the debtors, to the creditors who have registered orders to pay, and to the mortgagees. The bailiff should give a notice of this summons to the real property's registry within eight days. The summons must state the date of the hearing during which the observations about the particulars of the sale if any, will be decided upon, and the date of the sale (Article 418 C.Civ.Proc.).

289. The deposit of the list of the conditions of the sale must be published in a daily newspaper and on the stand of publications in the court within eight days of the last summons (Article 421 C.Civ.Proc.).

290. Objections to the proceedings or observations about the conditions of the sale must be raised, three days before the date of the hearing during which they shall be decided upon (Articles 418/5–422 C.Civ.Proc.).

291. The sale of real property seized is made at a public auction by the judge of execution assisted by the execution officer. The auction starts at the reserve price. The bids may be offered by anyone who wants to buy and is legally eligible to do so. The length of time during which the bidding may take place is three minutes. If a bid is offered and stays for three minutes without a successive bid higher than the precedent, the last bid is accepted. The bidder then has to pay 'at least one-fifth of the bid and the execution's expenses (Article 440/1 C.Civ.Proc.) immediately.

292. There is an opportunity for anyone to offer a price raised by one-tenth than the accepted bid if the bidder whose bid has been accepted did not immediately pay the entire price.

If a bid of a price 10% higher is offered, the judge postpones the hearing. There will be a new auction on the basis of the new reserve price. In the new auction, no one may offer a bid unless it is accompanied by the payment of the amount of money he offers as a price.

293. Objections to the proceedings concerning the publicity or the notifications for the auction should be made three days before the day on which the auction will take place. The judge of execution decides on these objections before the auction (Article 432 C.Civ.Proc.).

294. The sale is recorded in a judgment of adjudication. This judgment will not be rendered until the entire price, and the expenses of the execution have been paid. This judgment is entered into the public registry by the court's clerk (Article 447/1 C.Civ.Proc.).

295. The judgment of adjudication may be appealed for nullity of the procedure of the auction or for nullity of the judgment of adjudication itself. The time limit of appeal is five days from the day of the judgment (Article 541 C.Civ.Proc.).

§6. Distribution of the Proceeds of the Enforcement

296. Egyptian law organizes the procedures of the distribution of the proceeds of the enforcement in Articles 469–486 (C.Civ.Proc). The distribution takes place only if there is more than one creditor involved in the execution and the proceeds are not enough to cover the debts for the payment of which the property has been seized and sold (Article 471 C.Civ.Proc.). The procedures of the distribution are not followed if the creditors and the debtor agreed on the form of distribution (Article 473 C.Civ.Proc.).

In case of non-agreement, the proceeds are deposited with the court and distributed under the supervision of the judge of execution. The proceeds are distributed according to a procedure called 'order' (Article 474 C.Civ.Proc.).

The mortgages are paid first in chronological order, and then the residue is shared among the unsecured creditors.

Chapter 3. Recognition and Enforcement of Foreign Judgments

297. Judgments in civil and commercial cases rendered by foreign courts are not recognized or enforced in Egypt unless an Egyptian court grants it an 'exequatur' which entails the recognition of the foreign judgment and makes it enforceable within Egyptian territory (Article 296 C.Civ.Proc.).

The Egyptian court which has jurisdiction for the action in exequatur is the Tribunal of Grand Instance located at the place where the enforcement of the foreign judgment will be executed (Article 297 C.Civ.Proc.).

The proceedings of this action are the ordinary adversary proceedings (Article 297 C.Civ.Proc.). The action may be raised by any party having an interest in enforcing the judgment.

298. In the absence of an international treaty, the court shall not grant the recognition or the enforcement of a foreign judgment unless the following conditions have been fulfilled:

(1) That the foreign court that rendered the judgment had jurisdiction of the subject matter of the dispute, according to international rules of jurisdiction applied in its law, and that the case is not under the jurisdiction of the Egyptian courts.
(2) That the parties have been duly summoned and legally represented.
(3) That the judgment may not be appealed according to the law of the court which rendered it.
(4) That the judgment is not in contradiction with any judgment rendered by an Egyptian court.
(5) That the judgment is not contrary to public order or to morality in Egypt.

According to Article 296 (C.Civ.Proc.), if the there are other conditions for the recognition or execution of an Egyptian judgment required by the law of the country of the foreign judgment, the Egyptian court does not issue the exequatur unless these conditions have been fulfilled.

299. The court, in action for exequatur, has no power to re-examine the conflict between the parties on merits.

The judgment on exequatur may be appealed according to ordinary rules, and the decision on appeal may be challenged by cassation.

Part X. Arbitration

Chapter 1. Introduction

300. Arbitration in Egypt is governed by the Arbitration Law in Civil and Commercial Matters No. 27/1994 (Arb.L.). This law is inspired by the United Nations Convention on International Commercial Arbitration (UNICITRAL) rules, but its rules govern both internal and international arbitration.

The Egyptian Law of Arbitration applies even if the arbitration is based on an arbitral agreement concluded before the law entered into force.

Chapter 2. Arbitrability

301. The Egyptian Law of Arbitration No. 27/1994 applies to all arbitrations between public or private law persons.

Without prejudice to international conventions in force in Egypt, the law is applied to all arbitrations conducted in Egypt, and to arbitrations conducted abroad if the parties agree to subject it to the Egyptian Law of Arbitration (Article 1 Arb.L.).

Chapter 3. Arbitration Agreement and Party Autonomy

§1. General

302. In spite of its large field of application, the Egyptian Law of Arbitration No. 27/1994 applies only when there is an agreement of arbitration concluded by the free will of the parties (Article 4 Arb.L.). It does not apply to arbitration imposed by the law on the parties in a dispute.

303. According to Article 6 Arb.L., if the parties agree to subject their legal relationship to the provisions of a model contract, an international agreement or another document, the provisions of such document including those related to arbitration must be applied.

304. The Egyptian Law of Arbitration No. 27/1994 refers some arbitral matters to the Egyptian judiciary. Article 9 of the Egyptian Law of Arbitration No. 27/1994 determines the court which has jurisdiction according to the kind of arbitration. The provision of this article provides for a different rule with regards to whether the arbitration is international commercial arbitration or not:

(a) If it is international commercial arbitration, whether conducted in Egypt or abroad, the jurisdiction lies with the Cairo Court of Appeal unless the parties agree on the competence of another appellate court in Egypt.
(b) If it is not international commercial arbitration, the jurisdiction lies with the court having original jurisdiction over the dispute.

305. To be qualified as international commercial arbitration, the arbitration should be commercial and international:

(1) According to Article 2 Arb.L., arbitration is commercial if the legal relationship concerned is of an economic nature. It does not matter if it is contractual or non-contractual. The same article of the law gives some examples: the supply of commodities or services, commercial agencies, construction and engineering or technical know-how contracts, the granting of industrial, tourist and other licenses, technology transfer, investment and development contracts, banking insurance and transport operations, exploration and extraction of natural wealth, energy supply, the laying of gas or oil pipelines, the construction of roads and tunnels, the reclamation of agriculture land, the protection of the environment and the establishment of nuclear reactors. From these examples, it appears clearly that the law means by commercial, not only relationships between merchants, but also civil relationships of an economic nature.
(2) An arbitration is international, according to Article 3 (Arb.L.), if the subject matter relates to international trade in the following cases:
   (a) If the respective head offices of the parties are situated in two different countries at the time when the arbitral agreement was signed. If one of the

two parties has several business centres, the centre most linked to the subject matter of the arbitration is considered. If either of parties has no business centre, his usual place of residence should be considered.

(b) If the parties agree to resort to a permanent arbitral organization or arbitration centre situated in Egypt or abroad.

(c) If the subject matter of arbitration is linked to more than one country.

(d) If – at the time of the arbitral agreement – the respective head offices of the parties are located in the same country, and one of the following places is located outside this country:

  (i) The place of arbitration agreed upon.

  (ii) The place of performance of an essential part of the parties' commercial obligations.

  (iii) The place most linked to the subject matter of the dispute.

We have to note that the arbitration is considered international and commercial even if it is conducted in Egypt.

In both cases, the judicial court vested with jurisdiction shall continue to exercise exclusive jurisdiction until the termination of all arbitral proceedings (Article 9/2 Arb.L.).

306. According to Article 14 Arb.L., the judicial court referred to in Article 9 Arb.L. may, on the request of the interested party, order provisional or conservatory measures, whether before the start of the arbitral proceedings or during them.

§2. The Arbitration Compromise and the Arbitration Clause

307. The arbitral agreement is the agreement by which the parties agree to resort to arbitration as a means of resolving all or some of the disputes which arose or may arise between them relating to a certain legal relationship whether contractual or not (Article 10/1 Arb.L.).

This arbitral agreement may exist independently as an arbitration compromise or exist as a clause in a contract.

It exists independently when it regards disputes that occurred before the agreement.

In this case, the agreement must determine the matters included in the arbitration. This independent agreement may be concluded even when a judicial action has already been brought before a judicial court.

308. If the agreement exists as a clause of arbitration in a contract, it regards disputes which may arise in the future between the parties. In such case, the subject matter of the dispute should not be determined in the arbitral agreement, but must be determined in the request for arbitration.

The arbitration clause may appear in the form of a reference in the contract to a document containing an arbitral clause if the reference expressly considers that such clause is an integral part of the contract (Article 10 Arb.L.).

309. To be valid, the arbitral agreement (compromise or clause) should:

(a) be concluded by a person who has the capacity to dispose of his rights;
(b) have subject matter amenable to compromise (Article 11 Arb.L.);
(c) be concluded in writing. An oral arbitral agreement is void. No evidence may be accepted to prove it. The agreement is deemed in writing if it is included in a document signed by both parties or in letters, cables or other means of written communication exchanged between them (Article 12 Arb.L.).

§3. Arbitration Concerning Administrative Contracts

310. According to Article 1 Arb.L., the provisions of the law of arbitration shall apply to all arbitrations between public law or private law persons, whatever the nature of the legal relationship around which the dispute revolves.

By application to this article, the prevailing opinion is that arbitration is possible concerning contracts concluded by the government or a public juristic person, whether civil or administrative contracts.

311. In 1997, the legislator added to Article 10 Arb.L. a new amendment stating that 'for litigation about administrative contracts the arbitral agreement should be concluded after the approval of the competent minister or the person who is exercising his authority over the public juristic person. No delegation is permitted in this matter' (Article 10/2 Arb.L. added by Law No. 9/1997).

Without this approval, the arbitral agreement concerning an administrative contract is void.

When this arbitral agreement is approved, this approval by the concerned authority implies a waiver of the state of its judicial immunity regarding the enforcement of the arbitral award.

§4. Legal Effects of the Arbitral Agreement

312. The arbitral agreement has two legal effects:

(1) The right of each party to resort to arbitration.
(2) The lapse of the right of the party to resort to a judicial state court.

These two effects are effective even before the arbitrators have been nominated.

313. If, after the arbitral agreement, either party raises an action before the judicial state court, this action is not admissible, according to Article 13 Arb.L:

> A court, seized with a dispute in respect of which an arbitral agreement exists, must rule the case non-admissible if the defendant invokes a plea of non-admissibility before submitting any request or defence in the case.

The raising of a judicial action does not prevent the arbitral proceedings from commencing or continuing and does not prevent the Arbitral Tribunal from rendering the arbitral reward.

§5. Competence of Competence

314. The principle 'competence of competence' means that the Arbitral Tribunal is the sole organ to decide about its competence. It is a new concept in Egyptian law.

According to Article 22 Arb.L., the Arbitral Tribunal is empowered to rule on motions related to its non-competence, including motions based on the absence of an arbitration agreement, its expiry or nullity or its failure to include the subject matter of the dispute.

315. This motion of incompetence must be invoked no later than the time of submission of the Respondent's Statement referred to in paragraph 2 of Article 30 Arb.L. But if the motion is based on the fact that the arbitration agreement does not include matters raised by the other party, it should be invoked immediately; otherwise, the right to invoke it collapses.

The appointment or participation in the appointment of arbitration shall not disentitle the party from involving the motion of non-competence.

Anyhow, the Arbitral Tribunal may always accept a motion of non-competence after the time limit, if it deems that the delay to invoke the motion has been for an acceptable reason (Article 22/2 Arb.L.).

Chapter 4. Arbitral Tribunal

§1. Nomination of the Arbitrators

316. The Arbitral Tribunal should be composed of an odd number of arbitrators (Article 10/2 Arb.L.). Arbitrators are chosen by the mutual consent of the parties, either in the arbitration agreement or in a subsequent independent agreement. If the parties did not agree about the number of arbitrators, the tribunal shall be composed of three arbitrators (Article 1/1 Arb.L.).

Parties may nominate the arbitrators or choose a third person to nominate them, or agree upon the manner by which the arbitrators will be chosen. This person may be a juristic person.

317. In default of agreement by the parties, the arbitrators are chosen by the judicial court.

Article 17 Arb.L. determines the steps by which arbitrators are chosen by the court as follows:

(a) If the Arbitral Tribunal is composed of a sole arbitrator, the court shall appoint him.
(b) If it is composed of three arbitrators, each party shall appoint one arbitrator, and the appointed arbitrators shall appoint the third one. If any of the parties fail to appoint his arbitrator within thirty days from being requested to do so by the other party, or if the two arbitrators fail to appoint the third arbitrator within thirty days after their appointment, the court shall appoint the unnominated arbitrator on the request of the interested party.
(c) The arbitrator appointed by the two arbitrators or by the court shall preside the tribunal.

318. In nominating the arbitrator, the court must take into consideration the conditions required by the law and those agreed upon by the parties. Its decision may not be challenged.

319. The arbitrator, whether appointed by the parties, by the other arbitrators or by the court, must accept his mission. This acceptance should be in writing (Article 16/3 Arb.L.).

If the arbitrator accepts his mission, he is under an obligation to continue his mission until its end.

320. Because the arbitrator is exercising judicial power, the law has determined certain conditions for anyone to be an arbitrator:

(1) The arbitrator must be a natural person enjoying his full civil rights. A minor, a person who is deprived of his civil rights by a judgment for a felony or misdemeanour contrary to morality or by the effect of a judgment of his bankruptcy, may not be an arbitrator unless he has been rehabilitated (Article 16 Arb.L.).
(2) The arbitrator must be neutral and independent of the parties. According to Article 16/3 (Arb.L.) when the arbitrator accepts the mission entrusted to him, he must disclose any circumstances which cast doubts on his independence or neutrality.

321. An arbitrator may be a man or a woman, an Egyptian or a foreigner. The Egyptian Law of Arbitration No. 27/1994 declares expressly that 'the arbitrator need not be of a specific sex or nationality' (Article 16/2).

322. Besides these conditions required by law, the parties may add any additional condition not contrary to law or to public order. They may require, for example, that the arbitrator should be a woman or an Egyptian or of a certain profession or a certain age.

§2. Challenge of Arbitrators

323. The arbitrator may be challenged if there is serious doubt on his neutrality or independence. But, if a party appoints an arbitrator or participates in his appointment, he may not challenge him unless he has discovered the reason for challenge after such appointment (Article 18 Arb.L.).

The party may not challenge the arbitrator whom he had previously challenged in the same arbitration (Article 19/2 Arb.L.), even if he indicates in the new challenge a new reason.

324. The request of challenge is submitted to the judicial court referred to in Article 9 Arb.L. within fifteen days from the date the party has known of the appointment of the arbitrator and the reason of challenge (Article 19/1 Arb.L. amended by Law No. 8/2000).

The claim of challenge of an arbitrator does not have a suspensive effect on the proceedings of arbitration.

If the claim of challenge is accepted, the arbitration proceeding already conducted, including the award, is deemed null and void (Article 19/3 Arb.L.).

§3. Termination of the Arbitrator's Mission

325. Usually, the arbitrator performs his mission until its ends by rendering the award. But sometimes his mission ends before this time. This happens when the arbitrator resigns with the approval of the parties, or when the parties agree to discharge him.

It may happen that the arbitrator becomes unable to perform his mission due to illness, or fails to perform it, or he may interrupt his performance in a manner which leads to unjustifiable delay in the arbitration proceedings. In these cases, any party may then ask the judicial court referred to in Article 9 to terminate his mission (Article 20 Arb.L.).

326. When an arbitrator's mission is terminated, a substitute shall be appointed in his place in the same way as the precedent arbitrator was nominated (Article 2 Arb.L.).

Chapter 5. Interim Measures and Preliminary Awards

327. The norm is for the arbitral tribunal to issue one award on the merits of the case, terminating the whole dispute, and deciding on all claims submitted to it. However, the tribunal may issue an award terminating dispute, without deciding on the merits. On the other hand, the arbitral tribunal may issue awards that do not terminate the entire dispute. These may be awards relating to procedures as if they were to appoint an expert or to stop the dispute or to interrupt it; or they may be temporary awards, i.e., conclusive in the temporal request.

In addition to the awards, the tribunal may also issue orders or decisions.

§1. Partial Award

328. The awards that do not terminate the entire dispute may be conclusive in some merits. These awards are called partial awards. Article 42 of the Egyptian Arbitration Law expressly stipulates: '*The arbitral tribunal may issue partial or interim awards before issuing the final arbitral award which terminates the entire dispute*'.

Partial award is needed in some disputes, particularly in construction disputes where the arbitration takes place while the contractor continues to work. A partial judgment in construction arbitration may concern requests for delay, change orders issued by the employer, or the quantification of the works performed. The partial award shall contain specifically the claim or part of the claim it decides on, noting that the Tribunal continues to consider the remaining matters.

It is noted that a partial award is an award on merits rather than a temporal award. It decides on only part – not all – of the matters of a dispute before the arbitration, and the arbitral tribunal continues to consider the remaining matters. Therefore, the partial award does not terminate the tribunal's mandate. It is also noted that, despite the continuing mandate of the tribunal to consider the remaining issues, the tribunal exhausts its mandate in the matters decided in the partial award. The tribunal has no right to reconsider the matters already decided in its partial award.

The exercise by the arbitral tribunal of its authority to render partial awards does not require the parties' authorization. However, the parties may agree to deny such authority. In this case, it shall refrain from making any partial award.

§2. Preliminary Arbitration Award

329. The Egyptian Arbitration Law did not mention the possibility of the arbitral tribunal issuing preliminary awards.

Despite this deficiency, there is no doubt that the arbitral tribunal has the power to make preliminary awards in accordance with the Egyptian Arbitration Law. The law referred to some of the preliminary awards, such as the award of deferral of defences relating to the non-competence of the Tribunal (Article 22/1 and 22/2), and the award of appointing one or more experts (Article 36/1).

The preliminary award is characterized by being an award that does not terminate the dispute, in whole or in part, nor is it made in response to a temporal claim. It is intended to prelude the issuance of an objective award or temporal.

The law did not provide a form of preliminary award. Therefore, it can be issued in the form of a decision of the tribunal evidenced in the minutes of the hearing. It may also be issued in the form of an independent award signed by the majority of the tribunal. The preliminary award may be issued by the President of the tribunal if authorized by law.

§3. Temporal or Expedited Arbitration Award

330. The jurisprudence was that the agreement on arbitration did not grant the arbitral tribunal the power to issue interim judgments. It does not have the right to appoint a guard over the property in dispute, to control the termination of the guard against him or to replace the guard. An arbitration agreement only authorizes the arbitral tribunal to render a judgment in the merits of the dispute. The provision of an urgent judgment, which is the task of the courts of the state, does not prevent the agreement on arbitration without resorting to it to exercise its authority in this regard. However, some jurisprudence was of the opinion that if the parties expressly agreed to the jurisdiction of the arbitral tribunal to hear expeditious proceedings relating to the substantive dispute that the Tribunal is considering, it would have jurisdiction over that of the courts of the State.

However, modern jurisprudence has taken another view that the arbitration agreement empowers the arbitral tribunal not only to issue a judgment in the matter but also to issue temporary judgments before ruling on the subject. This trend was taken by the Egyptian Arbitration Act, which provided that 'the arbitral tribunal may render provisional provisions … before the final judgment of the entire adversary is rendered'. (Article 42 of the Arbitration Act). In this provision, the Egyptian legislator allowed the arbitral tribunal the power to issue temporary (urgent) judgments such as a court order or a judgment on temporary maintenance, before the arbitral tribunal issues its judgment on the matter.

The arbitral tribunal shall have such power whether the parties agree to authorize such authority or have not agreed. Their agreement to arbitrate in a particular dispute means that the arbitrators have the power to adjudicate the subject matter of the dispute and to issue expeditious interim judgments in accordance with their substantive jurisdiction. It is noted, however, that if the parties agree not to give the arbitral tribunal the power to issue interim judgments, the Tribunal may not issue any provision.

There are several conditions for the arbitral tribunal to issue a provisional ruling relating to the dispute:

(1) A Party shall submit a request to the Tribunal to judge the timely action required. The Tribunal may not decide on its own motion, and the application shall be submitted to the arbitral tribunal, and substantive motions shall be submitted to it. It can be submitted at any stage of the proceedings before the

case is reserved for judgment. A copy of this request must be sent to the other party in order to meet the principle of confrontation.

(2) The conditions of an urgent case shall be met. There must be a probability of the existence of the substantive right or legal status, and that there is urgency in the sense that there is a fear of the possibility of damage to the substantive right or legal status – if it exists – if the plaintiff does not receive the required time protection.

(3) The arbitral proceedings have commenced: the arbitral tribunal shall have this power only after the commencement of arbitration proceedings before it. Therefore, before the commencement of arbitral proceedings, the jurisdiction of the State Court (which is determined by Article 9 of the Arbitration Law) shall be the sole jurisdiction of rendering urgent judgments.

The authority of the arbitral tribunal to adjudicate the urgent request shall be the same as that of the State judge when adjudicates an expedited case and shall comply with the limitations to which the emergency jurisdiction of the State is subject. The arbitral tribunal, which issues the judgment, cannot affect the subject of the right. The documents and evidence provided by the litigants shall be examined in a superficial manner, which is sensitive to what is likely at first glance to be the right aspect of the urgent demand. If the Tribunal finds that the evidence and documents provided are not sufficient to indicate the probability of the substantive right claimed in the arbitration proceedings and that this presence is seriously disputed, it rejects the temporary request.

The arbitral tribunal has full power to modify the provisional request. It does not comply with the defendant's request to take action to protect its right of temporary protection but has the power to determine what is necessary to achieve such protection. The arbitral award shall be issued as the arbitrators' judgments are issued; A copy of it shall be delivered to each of the parties, and the original of the judgment shall be filed, as provided by law for the arbitrators' judgments.

§4. Interim Measures

331. Prior to the promulgation of the Arbitration Law, the jurisprudence established that the arbitral tribunal could not issue temporary injunctions even if the parties agreed to authorize such authority, on the basis that the imperium authority is only for the judges of the State. The arbitrator does not have the power of Imperium. The jurisprudence added that the temporary injunctions are issued without confrontation, and the arbitrators may not violate the principle of confrontation.

However, the modern trend, which was adopted by the Egyptian Arbitration Law in Article 24, allows the arbitral tribunal to issue such orders if the parties agree to give them such power. According to the first paragraph of this article: '*1. The parties to arbitration may agree that the arbitral tribunal may, at the request of one of them, order either to take whatever provisional or conservatory measures it deems the nature of the dispute requires, and request adequate security to cover the expenses of the measures ordered*'. By this provision, the law confers upon the arbitral tribunal an authority to issue an order for a temporary or provisional measure.

For example, the arbitral tribunal may authorize one of the parties to place the goods in dispute, which are under the hands of the requester, in a safe place, to authorize him to sell them in the market if they are damaged over time, or to order the suspension of liquidating a letter of guarantee. However, the arbitral tribunal may not issue an order to sign a provisional seizure on movables at the place of the debtor or on the debtor's debt with third parties. The issue of provisional seizure or of any measure of coercive enforcement is issued only by the judge.

The provision of Article 24 of the Arbitration Law does not preclude the parties to the arbitration agreement from resorting to the jurisdiction of the State to order an interim measure. The state court order referred to in Article 9 of the Arbitration Law may order the temporary order whether before or during the commencement of arbitral proceedings or during the pandect thereof (Article 14 Arb.L).

The recourse to the jurisdiction of the State shall not be considered to be a waiver of the arbitration agreement, even if the required provisional measure may be ordered by the arbitral tribunal.

An order may only be made against another party in the arbitral dispute. The arbitral tribunal may not issue a temporary order against a third party, as it has no power over third parties to the dispute.

According to the Egyptian Arbitration Law, the order must satisfy the following conditions:

(1) That parties to the arbitration shall expressly agree to give the arbitrators that power. This agreement may be stated in the arbitration agreement or in a subsequent agreement concluded even after the commencement of the arbitral proceedings.
(2) That arbitral proceedings have commenced before the Tribunal.
(3) That one of the parties to the arbitration has required to issue the order. The arbitrator may not issue a temporary order on his own.
(4) That the measure to be ordered shall be a temporary or a precautionary measure, as is the case with the order to deposit the goods in dispute in a public depository. Requests for evidence, such as a request to compel the opponent to submit a document under his hand is not accepted.

    Article 26 of the new rules of the Cairo Regional Center contained examples of temporal measures that the arbitral tribunal could order in an arbitration conducted in accordance with the Arbitration Law of 27/1994.

    It has been ruled that the arbitrator may not impose a threatening fine for each day on which the sentenced person is delayed from carrying out the arbitrator's orders. Neither the Egyptian Arbitration Law nor the rules of the Cairo Arbitration Center authorize such authority. Article 24 of Egyptian Arbitration Law does not grant the arbitrator more power than issuing provisional or reservation orders, and Article 26 of the Centre's rules speak of orders of a conservatory nature.
(5) That the requested measure shall be required by the nature of the dispute. The arbitrators should exercise their power to the minimum extent required by the nature of the dispute.
(6) That the general conditions for issuance of a temporary order shall be met. Namely, that there is a probability that the right or legal status in question

exists and that there is an urgent need to obtain the order for fear of the possibility of damage to the right – if exists, that the order required is not prejudicial to the subject, and that the objective of the order required would be reached only without confrontation.

(7) That the subject matter of the dispute shall be within the jurisdiction of the arbitral tribunal. If it is not permissible to arbitrate it, or is outside the scope of the arbitration agreement, the arbitral tribunal may not order the provisional measure required.

The competence to issue an order for a temporary measure – in accordance with the explicit provision of Article 24 – shall be to the arbitral tribunal, and not to the Chairman of the Tribunal (in case of multiple arbitrators). The Chairman of the Tribunal alone may not issue the order.

The arbitral tribunal does not comply with condition required by the procedural law (art. 194) that a judge may not issue orders except in the cases provided for in the law since there is no similar disposition in the Arbitration Law. Moreover, the competence of the arbitral tribunal derives from the agreement of the parties. It is bound only by the provisions of the Arbitration Law or the parties' Agreement.

The Arbitral Tribunal shall not abide in its ruling on the subject matter of the dispute by what it has directed in its opinion in issuing the temporary order.

The order shall be issued by a temporary or provisional measure in the form of a decision of the arbitral tribunal (not in the form of an order on a petition), and it shall not be reasoned. No appeal or challenge of nullity to it shall be accepted. However, the arbitral tribunal may modify, terminate or suspend the provisional or discretionary measure ordered by it, without being bound by reasoning its decision.

In accordance with Article 24/1 of the Egyptian Arbitration Law, the arbitral tribunal may demand from the person in favour which the order was issued the presentation of an adequate guarantee to cover the expenses of the measures it orders if the agreement of the parties confers such power on it.

Usually, the person against whom the order is issued executes it voluntarily in compliance with the Tribunal's order. If he fails to do so, the arbitral tribunal may, at the request of the other party, authorize him to take the necessary measures to implement it. If the execution of the order requires action by the person which the order was issued against him, and he did not take the necessary action, the person in whose favour the order was issued has the right to demand compensation for the damage caused by the non-implementation. And the same situation if the implementation of the order may be executed only by taking action against the person against whom the order was issued. In such a case, a person in whom favour the order was issued may obtain from the President of the Court referred to in Article 9 of the Arbitration Law, an order of execution for the execution to be carried out in force. (Article 24/2 Arb.L) and shall have this right without the need for permission from the arbitral tribunal.

Chapter 6. Conduct of Arbitral Proceedings

§1. Non-conformity to the State Court Proceedings

332. Arbitration proceedings do not conform to state court's proceedings. The principle, adopted by Egyptian law, is that the parties themselves have the right to agree on the procedures to be followed by the Arbitral Tribunal. They may draw up special procedures even if these procedures do not conform to procedures prescribed by the Arbitration Law. Parties are bound only to respect in the procedures agreed upon the fundamental principles of justice such as the equality between parties, the respect of the right of defence. The Egyptian Law of Arbitration No. 27/1994 includes a special article for the principle of equality, and for the right of defence. According to Article 26: 'The parties to arbitration shall be treated on an equal footing, and each party shall be accorded a fair and full opportunity to present his claims.'

The parties may also, instead of drawing up the procedures, agree to subject the procedures of arbitration to the provisions in force in any organization or Center of Arbitration in Egypt or abroad.

333. In the absence of the agreement of the parties, the Arbitral Tribunal may adopt the arbitration procedures it deems suitable. But the Arbitral Tribunal must respect not only the fundamental principles of justice but also the provisions of the Egyptian Law of Arbitration No. 27/1994 (Article 25 Arb.L.).

§2. Egyptian Arbitration Law Procedures

I. Commencement of Proceedings

334. The arbitration proceeding is deemed to commence from the date the respondent receives the request for arbitration from the claimant unless the parties agree on another date (Article 27 Arb.L.), like the date of the first hearing.

II. Place of Arbitration

335. The parties have the right to agree on the place of arbitration, whether in Egypt or abroad. In the absence of such agreement, the Arbitral Tribunal determines the site of Arbitration with regard to the circumstances of the case and convenience for the parties. The Arbitral Tribunal always has the power to conduct some procedures such as hearing the parties or the witnesses, holding deliberations, in any place, it deems suitable (Article 29 Arb.L.).

III. Language of Arbitration

336. According to Article 29 Arb.L., arbitration should be conducted in Arabic unless another language or languages are agreed upon by the parties or decided by the Arbitral Tribunal.

The arbitral tribunal may require that all or some of written documents submitted in the case be accompanied by a translation in the language or in some or all languages used in the arbitration.

IV. The Claimant's Statement

337. The claimant's statement is a statement written by the claimant or his lawyer containing his name and address, the respondent's name and address, an explanation of the facts of the case, a definition of issues subject of dispute and his claims. This statement must be sent to the respondent and to each of the arbitrators within the time limit agreed upon by the parties or decided by the Arbitral Tribunal (Article 30 Arb.L.).

The claimant may modify or expand his claims, during the arbitration proceeding unless the Arbitral Tribunal decides not to accept such modification or expansion to avoid delaying its decision on the dispute (Article 32 Arb.L.).

If the claimant fails to submit his statement of claim within the time limit without an acceptable excuse, the Arbitral Tribunal should order the termination of the proceeding unless the parties agree otherwise (Article 34/1 Arb.L.).

V. Respondent's Memorandum of Defence

338. The respondent's memorandum is a memorandum written by the respondent or his lawyer containing his defence in reply to the statement of claim. The respondent may modify his defences or expand them during the arbitration proceeding unless the Arbitral Tribunal decides not to accept such modification or expansion to avoid delaying its decision on the dispute. He may also invoke in his memorandum any right arising from the subject matter of arbitration. This right of incidental claims from the respondent is available also at any stage of the proceedings if the Arbitral Tribunal finds circumstances justifying such delay.

If the respondent fails to submit a statement of defence within the time limit, the Arbitral Tribunal should continue the proceeding in spite of the lack of the defence of the respondent. But such continuation shall not be considered as approval by the respondent of the claimant's claim unless the parties agree otherwise (Article 34/2 Arb.L.).

VI. Submission of Documents

339. The claimant or the respondent may annex to his statement of claim or to his memorandum of defence, copies of the documents on which he based his claims or defences.

The Arbitral Tribunal may, at any stage of the proceeding, request from the party the submission of the originals of the documents (Article 30/3 Arb.L.).

Copies of documents and papers submitted to the Arbitral Tribunal should be sent to the other party (Article 31 Arb.L.). This is a simple application of the principle of adversary.

VII. Notification of Notices and Papers

340. According to Article 7/1 (Arb.L.), if no special agreement exists between the parties, any message or notice is delivered to the addressee either in person, at his office or residence. It may also be sent to him by mail to his mailing address known to both parties or indicated in the arbitral agreement or in the document stating the subject matter of arbitration. If any of these addresses cannot be traced, the message or notice is delivered by a registered letter to the addressee's last known residence, office, or mail-address (Article 7/2 Arb.L.).

341. This provision applies to all messages and notices, addressed between parties or to the Arbitral Tribunal, to a witness or to an expert. It applies to all messages or notices relating to the arbitration either before the start of the arbitration proceedings or during and after their termination.

But this provision does not apply to judicial notifications before the judicial court even if relating to the arbitration (Article 7/3 Arb.L.), such as the notification of a claim before the court to nominate an arbitrator or the notification of a claim of the nullity of the award.

VIII. Pleading Sessions

342. The Arbitral Tribunal may limit the proceeding to the submission of written memos and documents unless the parties agree otherwise (Article 33/1 Arb.L.).

But usually, the Arbitral Tribunal holds pleading sessions to enable the parties to explain their claims or defences and to present their arguments and evidence. The Arbitral Tribunal must notify the parties of the dates of the sessions in advance. But this obligation exists only for the first session.

The Arbitral Tribunal may use a clerk to write these minutes.

If any party fails to attend one of the sessions, the Arbitral Tribunal may continue with the arbitration proceedings (Article 35 Arb.L.).

Sessions of arbitration may be held even on holidays or after 7 p.m. Summary minutes of each meeting session should be recorded in a record, and a copy thereof should be delivered to each party (Article 33/3).

IX. The Discontinuation of the Arbitration Instance

343. The arbitration instance is discontinued for the same reasons as the judicial instance. The discontinuation of the arbitration instance is governed by the same rules, and raises the same effects, as the discontinuation of the judicial instance (Article 38 Arb.L.).

X. The Suspension of the Arbitration Instance

344. The arbitration instance may be suspended either by the consent of the parties or by a decision of the Arbitral Tribunal.

According to Article 46 Arb.L., the Arbitral Tribunal may suspend the instance in the course of the proceeding under two conditions (Article 46 Arb.L.):

(a) That a preliminary issue is raised before the Arbitral Tribunal which it has no jurisdiction, such as, if a document submitted to it is challenged for forgery or criminal proceeding has been taken concerning this document.
(b) That the Arbitral Tribunal deems that a decision on such issue is necessary for the resolution of the arbitration dispute.

Under these two conditions, the Arbitral Tribunal shall suspend the instance until a final judicial judgment is rendered.

Chapter 7. Evidence Before the Arbitral Tribunal

§1. General Rules

345. Facts submitted to the Arbitral Tribunal should be proved. The burden of proof lies upon the party who claims the existence of these facts as a basis of his action or his defence.

346. The arbitrator has the same power which the judge exercises on the different types of proof. He may, even ex officio, order the hearing of witnesses, ask a party to swear a completive oath, go to a site where the subject matter of arbitration is, interrogate the parties and request a party to present a certain document.

But, because the arbitrator does not have the judicial power of imperium, he may not compel a witness to attend or to answer questions which he has been asked. The witness is heard without taking an oath.

On the other hand, if the witness refrains from attending or declines to reply, the arbitrator may not fine the witness, he can only ask the President of the Court to fine him according to Articles 78, 80 Evidence Law (Article 37 Arb.L.).

§2. Expertise

347. The Arbitral Tribunal may appoint one expert or more to present a written or oral report about certain matters. Its decision must designate the mission entrusted to the expert. This decision has to be stated in the minutes of the session, and a copy of it sent to both parties (Article 36/1 Arb.L.). The expert does not take an oath before starting his mission (Article 33/2 Arb.L.).

348. The expert fulfils his mission in the presence of the parties. They should be notified of the date and place of the expert's work and should be enabled to present to him any information or documents related to the dispute. The parties should enable the expert to inspect and examine any documents, goods or other assets related thereto (Article 36/2 Arb.L.).

349. When the expert presents his report to the Arbitral Tribunal, the tribunal shall send a copy of the expert's report to each party, allowing him to express his view about the report. The tribunal may allow the parties to discuss with the expert the contents of his report (Article 36/2, 3 Arb.L.). In the session for the discussion of the report, each party may present his own expert to present an opinion on the matters contained in the report.

Chapter 8. Ending of the Arbitral Proceedings

350. The arbitration proceedings may end before rendering an award on the arbitration dispute. This takes place by an order issued either by the Arbitral Tribunal or by the President of the competent state court.

§1. Order of Ending by the Arbitral Tribunal

351. The Arbitral Tribunal issues an order of ending the proceeding in the following cases (Article 48 Arb.L.):

(a) When the parties agree to end the arbitration before the rendering of the award. This agreement contains the termination of the arbitration agreement, and consequently, the Arbitral Tribunal has no competence.
(b) If the claimant abandons the arbitration instance unless the defendant objects because of his serious interest in the continuation of the proceeding until the resolution of the litigation.
(c) If the parties settle the litigation by conciliation. In this case, the parties may request the statement of their settlement in the session's record.
(d) If the Arbitral Tribunal deems it useless or impossible to continue the arbitration proceeding.

§2. Order of Ending by the President of the State Court

352. According to Article 45 Arb.L., if the award is not rendered within the periods referred to in Article 44 Arb.L., each party may request the President of the court referred to in Article 9 Arb.L. to issue an order terminating the arbitration proceeding. In such a case, each party may bring his claim to the judicial court that has original jurisdiction (Article 45/2).

Chapter 9. Arbitral Award

§1. The Time Limit

353. The Arbitral Tribunal has to issue the final award ending the entire dispute within a time limit. Its judicial power is not permanent. The award rendered after the expiration of the time limit is void.

The time limit may be agreed upon by the parties either in the arbitration agreement or in a subsequent independent agreement. The parties may also agree to extend the time limit agreed upon. This extension may be by an express agreement, or tacitly. The most common example of the tacit agreement is the presence of the parties at a hearing before the Arbitral Tribunal after the extension of the time limit, without opposing its termination.

The extension of time limit, express or tacit, should be in writing.

354. In the absence of agreement about the time limit, the award should be rendered within twelve months starting from the commencement of the arbitration proceedings (Article 45/1 Arb.L.). According to Article 27 Arb.L., the proceedings are deemed commenced from the date the respondent receives the request for arbitration from the claimant unless otherwise agreed by the parties.

355. This time limit, either agreed upon or fixed by law, may be extended by the Arbitral Tribunal for another period not exceeding six months (Article 45/1 Arb.L.).

On the other hand, each of the parties may request the President of the judicial court referred to in Article 9 Arb.L. to issue an order extending the time limit to make it sufficient for rendering the award (Article 45/2 Arb.L.).

§2. Applicable Law

356. If the arbitrator has been expressly empowered by the parties to act as an amicable arbitrator, he issues the award on the merits according to the rules of justice and equity without being bound by the rules of law (Article 38/1 Arb.L.).

But, if he is not empowered with such authority, he should apply the legal rules agreed upon by the parties. The parties may agree to apply the law of a certain state. In this case, the Arbitral Tribunal applies the substantive rules of that law directly and not those referred by its rules of conflict of laws.

The parties may also agree to apply the rules embodied in a certain legal system, not related to the law of any state such as Islamic Law.

357. If the parties do not agree on the legal rules to be applied, the Arbitral Tribunal shall apply the substantive rules of the law it deems most closely connected to the dispute (Article 39/2 Arb.L.).

In all cases, the Arbitral Tribunal should take into account the terms of the contract disputed and the applicable commercial customs concerning the subject matter of the litigation (Article 39/3 Arb.L.).

§3. The Rendering of the Award

358. If the Arbitral Tribunal is composed of more than one, the award is rendered after deliberations conducted secretly by all the arbitrators. It is issued by the majority of opinions of the arbitrators composing the tribunal (Article 40 Arb.L.).

According to Article 24 Arb.L., the parties may agree that the Arbitral Tribunal can order either of them to take whatever provisional or conservatory measures it deems the nature of the dispute requires.

The award should be issued in writing (Article 43 Arb.L.). The Arbitration Law sets the formal elements for the drafting of the arbitration award. It should indicate the names of the arbitrators, their addresses, nationalities and qualities, the names of parties and their addresses, a copy of the arbitration agreement, a summary of the claims and documents presented, the date and place of the award, the decision of the tribunal and the reasons if required.

359. According to Article 43/2 Arb.L., the Arbitral Tribunal must indicate in the award the reasons for its decision unless the parties agree otherwise or the law applicable to the proceeding does not require these reasons.

The reasons – if required – should be sufficient and non-contradictory.

360. The award must be signed by the arbitrators. If some of the arbitrators refrain from signing, the signatures of the majority shall be sufficient. A statement of the non-signature of the minority and the reasons for their abstention should be indicated in the award (Article 43/1 Arb.L.).

361. The written award signed by the arbitrators is considered an authentic paper, and it has the power of evidence of authentic papers.

362. The award may not be published in whole or in part except with the approval of the parties to arbitration (Article 44/2 Arb.L.).

Each party has the right to receive from the Arbitral Tribunal an original of the award signed by the arbitrators who approved it (Article 44/1 Arb.L.).

363. The interested party must deposit the original of the award or a copy of it signed by the arbitrators who approved it in the language in which it was issued, or an Arabic translation thereof authenticated by the competent authority if it has been issued in a foreign language. This deposit is made to the clerk of the judicial court referred to in Article 9 Arb.L. The clerk shall state such deposit in a record, and each of the parties may obtain a copy of this record (Article 47 Arb.L.).

§4. The Discharging of the Arbitral Tribunal

364. The arbitration award discharges the Arbitral Tribunal, except for interpretation, for correction of material mistakes and for completion of an element of the claim or of a claim which has been omitted.

I. Interpretation of the Awards

365. If there is ambiguity in the decision of the Arbitral Tribunal, the interested party may request the Arbitral Tribunal to elucidate this ambiguity. This request must be presented within thirty days from receiving the award. The party requesting the interpretation must notify the request to other parties before presenting it to the Arbitral Tribunal. The request of interpretation is adversary.

366. The award of interpretation is issued under the same formalities as any award, but it should mention the decision requested to be interpreted and the ambiguous part which has been interpreted.

The Arbitral Tribunal must issue this award within thirty days from the date of the request, but it may extend this period by another thirty days if it deems such extension is necessary (Article 49 Arb.L.).

The award of interpretation is treated as complementary of the interpreted award and is subject to its means of challenge.

II. Correction of Material Mistakes

367. If the award contains any material mistake, whether in words or figures, the Arbitral Tribunal corrects this mistake ex officio or on the request of the interested party. The Arbitral Tribunal makes the correction without pleadings within thirty days of the issuance of the award or of the request for correction, but it may extend this period for another thirty days if it deems this necessary (Article 50 Arb.L.).

III. Completion of the Award

368. If the Arbitral Tribunal did not issue a decision on a claim or a part of a claim submitted to it, the interested party may, even after the expiry of the time limit for arbitration, request the same Arbitral Tribunal to issue an additional award on those claims overlooked by it. The request must be notified to the party before it is presented to the tribunal. This request is examined by the tribunal according to the same rules governing the arbitration proceeding and the applicable law. The tribunal should render its additional award within sixty days from the submission of the request. This time limit may be extended for another thirty days if it deems this necessary.

Chapter 10. Nullity of the Award

369. According to the Egyptian Law of Procedure before 1968, the arbitration might be challenged either by an appeal or by a petition for review or by an action of nullity. The Code of 1968 abolished the possibility of appealing the award and keeps the other two ways of challenge. But the Egyptian Law of Arbitration of 1994 abolished the petition for review of the award and kept only the action of nullity. Thus the arbitration award in Egyptian law may not be challenged except by the action of nullity. The text of Article 52/1 Arb.L. provides that arbitration awards issued in accordance with the provisions of this law may not be challenged by any of the means of challenge prescribed by the Code of Civil and Commercial Procedures.

§1. Cases of Nullity of the Award

370. The action on nullity of the award is admissible only in cases provided strictly by law. These cases are the following (Article 53 Arb.L.):

(a) If the parties have not agreed to arbitration, or if their agreement is void, avoidable or has expired.
(b) If at the time of the arbitration agreement, one of the parties had no capacity to conclude it according to the law governing his capacity.
(c) If any of the parties was not able to present his defence because he had not been properly notified of the appointment of the arbitrator or of the arbitral proceedings, or because of any other reason beyond his control.
(d) If the award did not apply, on the subject matter of the dispute, to the law agreed upon by the parties.
(e) If the Arbitral Tribunal has been constituted, or the arbitrators have been appointed contrary to the law or to the agreement of the parties.
(f) If the award rules on matters not included in the arbitration agreement.
(g) If the award – as a legal act – is null, or if there is a nullity in the proceeding which has affected the award. For the reason concerning the nullity in the proceeding, the party may not raise the action of nullity unless he has invoked this reason before the Arbitral Tribunal within the time limit prescribed in Articles 22/2 and 30/2 Arb.L.
(h) If the arbitration award violates public policy in Egypt. In this case, the court seized by the action on nullity should rule ex officio for the annulment of the award.

§2. Jurisdiction and Time Limit

371. The action on nullity lies in the jurisdiction of the Court of Appeal. It is an exception of the principle of double layer of jurisdiction.

Article 54/2 Arb.L. provides that:

> Jurisdiction over actions on the nullity of arbitral awards rendered in international commercial arbitration lies with the court referred to in Article 9 of this law. In other arbitrations, jurisdiction lies with the Court of Appeal to which the decisions of the court of original jurisdiction over the dispute are appealed.

372. The action on nullity must be raised within ninety days following the notification of the award to the other party.

The action is admissible even if the party involving nullity has waived his right to raise it as long as such waiver has happened before the award was issued (Article 54 Arb.L.).

Chapter 11. Enforcement of the Arbitration Award

373. The arbitration award has the authority of res judicata (Article 55 Arb.L.), but its execution may not be enforced without an order of exequatur from the judge.

The judge having jurisdiction to issue an order of exequatur of the arbitration award is the President of the court referred to in Article 9 Arb.L. or any of the judges of this court delegated by the President for this mission (Article 56/1 Arb.L.).

374. The raising of an action on nullity does not suspend the enforcement of the award. But, the court may order the suspension of the award, if the plaintiff requests it in his petition of nullity and such request is based upon serious grounds. If suspension is ordered, the court may require a certain guarantee to be presented by the plaintiff. When the court orders the suspension of enforcement, it must rule on the action of nullity within six months from the date of suspension (Article 57 Arb.L.).

375. The request for an exequatur is not acceptable if it has been submitted before the time limit of the action of nullity of the award.

To issue the order of exequatur, the judge should verify that the award:

(a) is not contrary to a judgment previously rendered by the Egyptian courts on the subject matter of the dispute;
(b) is not contrary to public order in Egypt;
(c) has been properly notified to the party against whom it was rendered.

376. According to Article 58 Arb.L. in its original text, the order granting the exequatur may not be challenged, but this disposition has been declared as unconstitutional by the judgment of the Egyptian Constitutional Court dated 6 January 2001 in Case No. 92/21 const. After this judgment, the order of issuing, or refusing the exequatur may be challenged before the court referred to in Article 9 Arb.L. within thirty days of the order (Article 58 Arb.L.).

377. The above-mentioned rules apply on arbitrations governed by the Egyptian Law of Arbitration No. 27/1994 which applies only to arbitrations conducted in Egypt and to arbitrations conducted abroad if the parties agree to subject it to the Egyptian Law of Arbitration.

The Recognition and Enforcement of Foreign Arbitral Awards to which the parties did not agree to apply the Egyptian Law of Arbitration are governed by the convention of New York. According to Article 1 of the Egyptian Law of Arbitration No. 27/1994, this law applies ‘without prejudice to the provisions of international conventions in force in the Arab Republic of Egypt’.

378. By Presidential Decree No. 171/1959 on 2 February 1959, Egypt joined the New York Convention of 1958 on the Recognition and Enforcement of Foreign Arbitral Awards. According to a ministerial decree of the Minister of Foreign Affairs, the convention was applied in Egypt on 8 June 1959.

379. It is useful to mention, in this regard, Article 3 of the New York Convention, which states that:

> Each contracting State shall recognize arbitral awards as binding and enforce them in accordance with the rules of the territory where the award is relied upon, under the conditions laid down in the following articles. There shall not be imposed substantially more onerous conditions or higher fees or charges on the recognition or enforcement of arbitral award to which this convention applies than are imposed on the recognition or enforcement of domestic arbitral awards.

Relying on this article, the Egyptian Court of Cassation has ruled that the recognition and enforcement of foreign awards even if the parties did not agree to apply Egyptian Law of Arbitration is governed by this Law because its rules are less onerous than those imposed by the rules disposed by Articles 296–299 of the Egyptian Civil Code of Procedure concerning the recognition and enforcement of foreign awards in Egypt (Cassan, 10 January 2005 Case No. 966/73.).

Selected Bibliography (In Arabic)

A. On Civil Procedure

Abdel Fattah, A. *Law of Egyptian Civil justice*. Cairo, 1991.
Abou El Wafa, A. *Law of Civil and Commercial Procedure*. Alexandria, 1986.
Alkasas, E. *Law of Civil and Commercial Procedure*. Cairo, 2005.
Al Sharkawi, A.M. *Civil and Commercial Procedure*. 1956.
Saad, E.N. *Judicial Private Law*. Alexandria, V.I-1974, V.2, 1980.
Seif, R. *Law of Civil and Commercial Procedure*. Cairo, 1969.
Ragheb, W. *Principles of Law of Civil Justice*. Cairo, 2001.
Waly, F. *Law of Civil Justice*. Cairo, 2009.
Waly, F. *Writings on Civil Justice and Arbitration (Notes and Articles Published in Legal Reviews, 1961–2014)*, Cairo, 2015.
Waly, F. *Treatise of Law of Civil Justice*. Cairo, 2017.
Younis, M.M. *Civil and Commercial Procedures*, 2015.

B. On the Enforcement of Judgments and Other Enforceable Instruments

Abou El Wafa, A. *Enforcement of Judgments*. Alexandria, 1982.
Abou Heif, A.H. *Ways of Enforcement and Protective Measures*. Cairo, 1923.
Fahmi M.H. *Enforcement of Judgments*. Cairo, 1951.
Seif, R. *Enforcement of Judgments*. Cairo, 1969.
Waly, F. *The Enforcement in Civil and Commercial Matters*. Cairo, 1995.
Younis, M.M. *Enforcement of Judgements*, 2013.
Zaghloul, A.M. *The Principles of Enforcement*. Cairo, 2002.

Index

The numbers here refer to paragraph numbers.

Action
 admissibility, 86–90
 capacity, 87
 collective, 85
 conditions, 84–85
 definition, 79–83
 interest, 86–90
 joinder, 183
 vexations, 91
Appeal
 conditions, 147–148
 counter-appeal, 151–153
 effects, 155–161
 incidental, 151, 153
 new claims, 157, 160
 new parties, 154
 proceedings, 149–154
 time limit, 146, 152, 153
Arbitration, 300–379
 administrative contracts, 310–311
 agreement, 302–315
 arbitrators, 316–326
 award, 327–331
 clause, 307–309
 competence, 314, 315
 compromise, 307–309
 ending of the proceeding, 350–352
 enforcement, 373–379
 evidence, 345–349
 international, 305, 371
 nullity, 369–372
 proceeding, 332–344
 provisional measures, 306, 331, 358
 state court jurisdiction, 312, 313, 330
Attorney at law (lawyers), 33–40
 admission, 33–35
Bailiff, 13, 41, 45–48, 125, 126, 127, 277, 278, 286, 288
Bar
 Court of Cassation, 35
 discipline, 39
 fees, 38
 immunities, 36
 incompatibilities, 37
 professional secrecy, 218

Cassation, 167–179
Claim, 92–94
 ancillary claims, 51, 62, 74, 93
Constitution
 oath, 231–237
 questioning of the parties, 227–230
 superior council of the judiciary, 12
 view of premises, 238–239
 witness, 219–226
 written proof, 209–213
Court
 administrative courts, 2, 3, 11, 12, 61, 62, 66
 commercial courts, 14
Court clerk, 122, 123, 225
Court of Appeal, 18, 21, 24, 39, 42, 67, 121, 149, 150, 156, 157, 159–161, 164, 271, 304, 371
Court of Cassation
 double layer of jurisdiction, 15
 Supreme Constitutional Court, 2
 Tribunal of Grand Instance, 16, 49
 Tribunal of Small Instance, 17, 50
 Tribunal of Urgent Matters, 51

Defence, 95–101, 338
Demurrer
 on the merits, 99, 108

procedural exception, 97–99

Enforcement, 261–299
distribution of proceeds, 296
enforceable instruments, 266–268
exequatur, 297–299
foreign judgment, 297–299
judge of execution, 263–264
security, 274
seizure, 272–295
Evidence
actio ad exhibendum, 218
admissibility, 206–208
burden, 204
expert, 240–249
inquiry, 222–226
oath, 231–237
questioning of the parties, 227–230
view of premises, 238–239
witness, 219–226
written proof, 209–213

Incidents, 182–196

Judge
appointment, 26–28
career, 29
discipline, 30–31
incompatibilities, 32
irremovability, 11
judge for urgent matters, 51–52
judge of execution, 263–264
Judgment
before the end of the process, 145
challenge of judgment, 144–181
correction of material mistakes, 36, 4 367
final, 148, 164, 271, 272, 330
in absence, 142
interpretation, 140
nullity, 144
on the merits, 138
reasons, 135, 137, 138, 150
res judicata, 90, 138, 170
supplement of judgment, 141
Jurisdiction
adjustment, 60–64
international jurisdiction, 68–78
matter jurisdiction, 49–52
resolution of conflicts, 65–67
territorial jurisdiction, 53–59
urgent matters, 51–52

Law officials, 41–48
See: Bailiff, Court clerk
Legal aid, 201–202
Legal costs, 197–200

Non-contentious matter, 251–255

Orders of payment, 256–260

Procedure, 4–8
adversary, 6–8
publicity, 9
Proceedings
conciliation, 111–116
default, 142–143
hearing, 128–132
jury, 130
lapse of procedural right, 110
nullity, 103–109, 148, 168
order upon request, 256–260
pleadings, 342
writ of summons, 268
see also, Appeal
Proof, *see* Evidence
Public minister, 12, 20, 174, 253

Time limit, 110, 140, 145, 146, 153, 164, 170–172, 174, 195, 222, 275, 278, 279, 295, 315, 337, 338, 353–355, 368, 370–272
Time limitation, 193
Treaty, 68–78, 298

www.ingramcontent.com/pod-product-compliance
Lightning Source LLC
Chambersburg PA
CBHW071349230926
51846CB00002B/485